Following Jesus

FOLLOWING JESUS

Biblical Reflections on Discipleship

N T Wright

First published in Great Britain 1994
Society for Promoting Christian Knowledge
Holy Trinity Church, Marylebone Road
London NW1 4DU

Second impression 1998

The author and publishers are grateful to Faber and Faber Ltd. for
permission to reproduce the extracts from 'The Journey of the Magi'
by T S Eliot from *The Collected Poems of T S Eliot 1909–1992*.

British Library Cataloguing-in-Publication Data

A catalogue record for this book is available from the British Library

ISBN 0-281-04805-3

Typeset by Tom Wright, Lichfield, using *Nota Bene* software

Printed in Great Britain by Biddles Ltd,
Guildford & King's Lynn

for the congregation of Lichfield Cathedral

Contents

PREFACE

The longer you look at Jesus, the more you will want to serve him in his world. That is, of course, if it's the real Jesus you're looking at. Plenty of people in the church and outside it have made up a 'Jesus' for themselves, and have found that this invented character makes few real demands on them. He makes them feel happy from time to time, but doesn't challenge them, doesn't suggest they get up and do something about the plight of the world. Which is, of course, what the real Jesus had an uncomfortable habit of doing.

I have written elsewhere about the search for Jesus (in my little book, *Who Was Jesus?* (SPCK, 1992), and in my forthcoming larger book, *Jesus and the Victory of God* (SPCK, 1995)). The present book is about the 'so what?' which necessarily follows on from that search. The New Testament writers were extremely interested in this question. In fact, the gospels themselves, which set out to tell their readers about Jesus himself, go about this task in such a way as to say to their readers: the ball is now in your court; the true Jesus is summoning you to follow him, to a life of discipleship. I suspect that we have yet to feel the full impact of the challenge the gospels present.

The following chapters started life as attempts to explore and expound that challenge from the pulpit. The first half of the book began as a series of sermons in Lichfield Cathedral, during Lent 1994, with the sixth and last being preached (as will be clear from its tone and content) on Easter Day. These sermons, each examining a particular New Testament book, aimed to provide a kind of aerial photograph or bird's-eye view of the book in question, so that one might see how the land lies. To change the image, I have supplied a kind of programme note for each book, so that, as with a symphony, one can listen out for the main themes. Each time, I draw particular attention to the way in which the writer points his readers to Jesus, as the focus of devotion and the inspiration for discipleship. Each writer talks about the life, death and resurrection of Jesus in order to encourage his readers to follow this Jesus wherever he leads. I have tried to think through what this might mean in terms of the present day.

The second half of the book ranges more widely over various topics which together inform, and set the context of, the biblical model of discipleship. Chapters 7, 8 and 12 were preached in Worcester College, Oxford, during the last two years of my chaplaincy there. Chapter 9 was preached in Pusey House, Oxford; Chapter 10 in Coventry Cathedral; and Chapter 11 in St Paul's Cathedral. I am grateful for the invitations to preach in these distinguished places, and for the welcome and hospitality I enjoyed.

All the chapters, not just those in the first half, should be treated as invitations to do some homework. They grew out of my reading of the Bible, and are intended to encourage hearers and readers to read it afresh for themselves. In the second half of the book, I follow the more conventional method of working from a fairly short passage, usually one which had been read in the course of worship. In the first half of the book, I am attempting to expound biblical books in their entirety. People do not always, perhaps, realize how natural and easy reading whole books of the Bible can be. You can read through Colossians quite slowly in about twelve minutes; you can get through Hebrews in under an hour. John may take longer, but time will quickly become a secondary consideration. I am convinced that using a lectionary – reading the Bible in little snippets – is a second-order activity; the primary activity ought to be reading the Bible in large chunks, to get its full flavour and thrust. One word of advice; try using a good modern translation that you haven't used before, to jolt you into seeing things in new ways. In this book, I have often simply used my own translation, with the same intent. Where I have used a modern translation, it is usually the New Revised Standard Version.

Many of the sermons – all those in the first Part, and Chapters 9 and 10 in the second – were preached in the context of the Eucharist, and some of the eucharistic references remain. This, I am again persuaded, is no bad thing. The visible word and the written word – or, if you like, the edible bread and the audible bread – go closely together, as they did for the two on the Emmaus Road in Luke 24. Following Jesus, after all, involves heart, mind, soul and strength. A church without sermons will soon have a shrivelled mind, then a wayward heart, next an unquiet soul, and finally misdirected strength. A church without sacraments will find its strength cut off, its soul undernourished, its heart prey to conflicting emotions, and its mind engaged in increasingly irrelevant intellectual games. This book is part of the attempt to address the first of these problems. Nowhere in it do I attempt to expound what I think is going on in the Eucharist itself. I made a small start in Chapter 11 of *The Crown and the Fire* (SPCK, 1992). But if these pieces suggest ways in which word and sacrament can be held firmly together, supplying together the context and the energy to enable us to follow Jesus, I shall be delighted.

It only remains to thank those who have helped this book on its way. I am deeply grateful to Keith Sutton, Bishop of Lichfield, for all his support, friendship, and inspiration; and to Tony Barnard, John Howe, Richard Ninis, and John Turner, my colleagues on the Cathedral Chapter, for their welcome, help and encouragement during my first months here. At SPCK, Philip Law has been a cheerful and wise editor; David Mackinder has applied his sharp eyes to the text with his usual efficiency. At home, my dear wife has, as always, carried a heavy load on my behalf; my children have put up with more disruption and dislocation in this last year than ever before. But the last word must go to those to whom this book is dedicated, the first hearers of Part I. The warmth of the welcome which they offered to their new Dean was truly wonderful; their enthusiasm for thinking fresh thoughts has been unbounded. I hope they will receive this little thank-offering as a small token of my heartfelt gratitude.

Tom Wright
Lichfield Cathedral
Trinity 1994

PART ONE

Looking to Jesus

'. . . let us run with perseverance the race that is set before us, looking to Jesus, the pioneer and perfecter of our faith, who for the sake
of the joy that was set before him endured the cross, disregarding its
shame, and has taken his seat at the right hand of the throne of God.
Consider him who endured such hostility against himself from sinners, so that you may not grow weary or lose heart.'

Hebrews 12.1–3

CHAPTER ONE

The Final Sacrifice: Hebrews

> We do not have a high priest who is unable to sympathize with our
> weaknesses, but we have one who in every respect has been tested
> as we are, yet without sin. Let us therefore approach the throne of
> grace with boldness, so that we may receive mercy and find grace
> to help in time of need. (Hebrews 4.15–16)

These are familiar words to many Christians. The old Anglican
Prayer Book used the phrase 'comfortable words' to describe words
full of comfort; and these words are, in that old sense, some of the
most comfortable to be had. But they come from the book which,
almost without rival in the New Testament, presents problems and
obscurities to the modern reader. The letter to the Hebrews is
undoubtedly the work of a learned and brilliant writer, and a
Christian of deep faith and devotion. But what on earth is it all about?

Contemporary Christians often feel Hebrews to be a strange and
difficult book. There are, I think, two reasons for this.

First, it seems to ramble about and discuss a lot of themes which
have never made it into the 'top ten' of Christian discussion topics. It
begins with a complex discussion of angels; continues with a treatment of what Psalm 95 really meant in talking about 'entering God's
rest'; moves on to Melchizedek; lists the furniture in the Tabernacle;
and ends with an exhortation to 'go outside the camp'. Well, you see
what I mean; were I a betting man, I would lay good odds that none
of my readers have found themselves discussing these things over the
breakfast-table within the last month or two. Small wonder that most
people don't get very far with Hebrews, or let it get very far with
them.

All right, there are bits that stand out as interesting and relevant.
There is the passage quoted above, which speaks of Jesus being tested
just as we are and so being able to sympathize with us. There is the

great passage about faith in chapter 11. There is the wonderful blessing at the end, which we often use, the one about 'the God of peace
who brought again from the dead our Lord Jesus, the great shepherd
of the sheep'. But the way Christians use these passages is rather like
putting in the thumb and pulling out a couple of obvious plumbs.
There comes a time for seeing what the rest of the pie is made of as
well.

The second reason the book is felt difficult is that it concentrates
on animal sacrifice. Most of us have never seen an animal being
killed, let alone sacrificed, and would be rather horrified if we did.
(For most cultures, at most periods in history, it would of course have
been extremely familiar.) So, when Hebrews goes on about sacrifice,
we feel it's in slightly bad taste. But the trouble doesn't stop there.
The word 'sacrifice' has then become a metaphor with a religious
colouring, and has been used to back up all sorts of appeals: to the
young, that they should go off and fight wars wished upon them by
the old; to women, that they should 'sacrifice' themselves for the sake
of husband or children; to Christian workers, who are asked to
'sacrifice' – i.e. to accept a ridiculously low salary – because
ordinary churchgoers don't want to give realistically towards their
support. We have, in short, become squeamish about real sacrifices,
and manipulative with metaphorical ones.

How then are we to approach Hebrews? And how does it help us
as we begin to think about following Jesus? I want to give you, in the
best preachers' fashion, three lines of thought which may open the
book up for us, not least in coming to the Eucharist.

First, Hebrews offers us *a compelling portrait of Jesus*. The passage with which we began, speaking of Jesus as the high priest who
can sympathize with our weaknesses, needs to be set within the total
sweep of the letter. Let me give you a bird's-eye view of it.

In chapter 1, Jesus is the Son of God, superior even to the angels.
There were some in the early Church who thought of Jesus as just a
special sort of angel; no, says the writer, he is of a different order of
being altogether. But at once, in case you should get the wrong idea,
chapter 2 emphasizes that Jesus is also totally and truly human. Please
note: not only *was* Jesus totally and truly human, he *still is*. One
writer described Hebrews' portrait of Jesus as 'our man in heaven'.
That is one of the major thrusts of the book – to emphasize that the
one who has sat where we sit, who has lived our life and died our

death, has now been exalted and glorified precisely as a human being. He hasn't, as it were, 'gone back to being just God again'. Chapter 2 closes with the first statement of our opening theme: because he himself was tested by what he suffered, he is able to help those who are being tested.

Then, in chapters 3 and 4, Jesus is the true Joshua; it's the same name, actually, in Hebrew and Greek. He is the one who leads the people of God into their true promised land. Then, in chapters 5, 6 and 7, he is the true high priest. That's where Melchizedek comes in. To understand this we need to take a step sideways for a moment.

It was a problem for the early Church that Jesus was from the house of David. It meant he was qualified to be Messiah, that is, King of Israel. But it disqualified him from being a high priest, who should have been from the house of Levi, a different tribe altogether. Hebrews points out that, in Psalm 110, the King is said to be a priest for ever, *according to the order of Melchizedek*, whose priesthood does not depend on ancestry but on the call of God alone. Jesus is not, then, a transient high priest, to be replaced by someone else. He remains a priest for ever. In other words, summing up where we've got to so far, Jesus, the Son of God, the truly human one, is leading his people to their promised land, and is available for all people and for all time as the totally sympathetic one, the priest through whom they can come to God. Following Jesus is the only way to go.

We then move into chapters 8—10, which speak of Jesus' sacrifice and the new covenant, to which we shall return. This leads us to the great list of the heroes of faith in chapter 11. There are lists like this in various Jewish writings; and the vital thing about the list is, who comes at the end? In one of the most famous lists, the one in Ecclesiasticus which begins 'Let us now praise famous men . . .', the answer is: the Aaronic high priest, in the Temple. The answer here, predictably, is: Jesus himself. In chapter 12.1-3 the writer issues an appeal which could stand as the key biblical text on the whole theme of 'following Jesus':

Since we are surrounded by so great a cloud of witnesses, let us also lay aside every weight and the sin that clings so closely, and let us run with perseverance the race that is set before us, looking to Jesus, the pioneer and perfecter of our faith, who for the sake of the joy that was set before him endured the cross, disregarding its shame, and has taken his seat at the right hand of the throne of God.

Consider him who endured such hostility against himself from sinners, so that you may not grow weary or lose heart.

The themes we have already looked at come to a head in this passage. Take them in reverse order: Jesus, the high priest, coming at the end of the great list of heroes. Jesus, the one who leads us into our promised land, the pioneer, the one who goes ahead to blaze the trail. Jesus, the truly human being, who has travelled the road of human suffering ahead of us. Jesus, now enthroned as Son of God. Jesus, therefore – as the final chapter, chapter 13, puts it – Jesus Christ, the same, yesterday, today and for ever; Jesus, the great shepherd of the sheep, the one brought again from the dead. That is the picture of Jesus which Hebrews offers us; it is the Jesus who will guide us through life, the Jesus who meets us today as we feast at his table, the Jesus who summons us gently but clearly to follow him. And at the heart of this picture we find the cross: the cross which Jesus endured on our behalf, which was the climax of his life of suffering and rejection, which was, as we shall see, the final sacrifice. This, then, is the first part of the bird's-eye view of Hebrews: a picture of the human high priest Jesus and his cross.

The second part of the bird's-eye view of Hebrews has to do with *a new reading of the Old Testament*. One of the reasons why people find Hebrews hard to understand is that the Old Testament isn't as well known today as it used to be. But even where it is, what this writer does *with* the Old Testament often seems very odd. In fact, once we grasp what's going on, it is really comparatively straightforward.

The point is this: he continually presents the Old Testament as *an unfinished story*, and shows that it invites and even requires a final chapter. My family and I have become quite familiar with the M40 motorway over the last year, driving frequently between Oxford and Lichfield. Yet only three or four years ago the M40 consisted of a longish road which came to a stop a few miles south of Birmingham. If you had driven up it, supposing you could have got on to it, you would have been going in the right direction; there would have been signs already in place, telling you that this road would take you to Birmingham and beyond; but you would get to a certain point and the road would stop. It required a final section, to get to its destination.

According to Hebrews, the Old Testament is like the M40 without its final section; and the final section, which gets you to your destination, is Jesus himself – specifically, the sacrifice with which he brings into being the new covenant. The argument of Hebrews runs like this: the Jewish scriptures are continually pointing beyond themselves to a further reality which they do not themselves contain. More particularly, they are pointing to a great act of salvation, of dealing with sin, which they do not themselves offer. This great act has now been accomplished in Jesus; and we must therefore follow this Jesus. Let me take you through this argument, as it appears in the five steps of the letter.

First (chapter 1), the Old Testament speaks of angelic beings all becoming subservient to someone greater than themselves. Who can this be but the Messiah, the Son of God? Second (chapter 2), the Old Testament speaks of the whole world as subject to the rule of the human race; but this clearly isn't true in general; it has come true in the enthronement of the man Jesus. Third (chapters 3—4), the Old Testament speaks of a time of 'rest', of entering the promised land, even in writings which were written long after the entry into Canaan. There must be a different, more permanent rest, still to come. Fourth (chapters 5—7), the Old Testament speaks of a king who is also a priest. How can this be, within the categories of Jewish priesthood? Answer: it can only be so in the person of Jesus. Fifth, and finally (chapters 8—10), the Old Testament speaks of a new covenant, in which sins will finally be dealt with once and for all. This clearly implies that the old covenant, the agreement between God and Israel, was a temporary measure designed to lead to the eventual solution. At each stage, Hebrews argues, the Old Testament points beyond itself to Jesus and his cross as the fulfilment of the age-long plan of the one true God. The unfinished story has come to its fulfilment. Now you can see clearly who you have to follow.

Within the letter in its original context, this argument is pretty clearly designed to persuade Jewish Christians that they can't go back to non-Christian Judaism, perhaps under the threat of persecution. Now that they have the fulfilment, they mustn't go back to the preparatory stage. For us today that isn't likely to be a problem. But the argument does two things for twentieth-century Christians in the modern West. First, it gives us a perspective on the Old Testament, which is no bad thing in itself. Second, it reminds us forcibly that what God did in Jesus Christ was not an odd, isolated incident, a one-off invasion into the world. It was the climax of his long plan. Our faith, and our discipleship, do not rest upon an oddity, but upon the rock-solid plan of the Lord of history. When we grasp the cross, we are not clutching at a straw but standing on a rock. When we celebrate the Eucharist, we are taking our place within God's history.

A compelling portrait of Jesus; a new reading of the Old Testament. Thirdly and finally, Hebrews offers us *Jesus the Final Sacrifice*. How are we to get at this notion, at once so central and (to us) so opaque? Let me suggest two ways in towards the heart of it.

First, sacrifice is part of what it means to be truly human. Humans were made, as Hebrews says, to be under God and over the world. The temptation we humans face, which Jesus faced in the wilderness, is to snatch at the world to use it for our own pleasure or glory. But when we bring a symbol of the created world before the creator God in gratitude and offering, we are symbolically saying that he is the creator, and that we have no rights over creation independently of him. To that extent, sacrifice is the natural and appropriate human activity.

Second, sacrifice (as the anthropologists and psychiatrists have been telling us for some time) lies deep within the human awareness that things which are wrong have to be put right; and the way in which they are put right involves the *conscience* and the *whole life* of those involved. There is an irony here. A generation ago, liberal thought managed to get rid of sin; and, with sin, most theories of atonement were dismissed as odd and unnecessary. But in our own generation we have rediscovered guilt; we have shame and violence in plenty; we have alienation at all levels. And we don't know what to do with it, either at a personal or at a corporate level. Cleansing of the conscience is what is required; and the only way to do that is by the total offering of the human life to God.

But that total offering isn't something we can do for ourselves. If we try, we are merely trying to pull ourselves up by our own boot-straps. That's why the Old Testament, pointing forwards, teaches that God himself provides the sacrifice necessary to cleanse the conscience. And that's why the letter to the Hebrews argues that the sacrifice of Jesus himself is the one true sacrifice towards which all others point. The blood of bulls and goats, it says, can't really take away sins; they point forwards to the one sacrifice that can and does purify us, that washes our consciences clean.

Look at it from the viewpoint of a wider biblical theology. God chose the human race to be the priests of all creation, offering up creation's worship to him and bringing his wise order to it. When humans sinned, God chose the nation of Israel to be the priests of the human race, offering up human praise, and putting into operation God's solution to the problem of sin. Israel herself, however, was sinful; God chose a family of priests (the sons of Aaron) to be priests to the nation of priests. The priests themselves failed in their task; God sent his own Son to be both priest and sacrifice. The inverted pyramid of priesthood gets narrower and narrower until it reaches one point, and the point is Jesus on the cross. The sacrifice of Jesus is the moment when the human race, in the person of a single man, offers itself fully to the creator.

The result is that now at last true human life is possible. Now at last consciences can be washed clean. It is ironic that, within what appears at first blush to be one of the most obscure books of the New Testament, we find the news that millions in our society are desperate to hear: the news that the things which trouble us most deeply can be washed away through the blood of Christ. Following Jesus appears hard because we feel we start off with a deficit to wipe off. Hebrews not only summons us to follow Jesus; it explains that the moral deficit is already dealt with. This book may be old, but that news in particular is as up-to-date as tomorrow morning's newspaper.

So the book of Hebrews offers us, quite simply, Jesus. It offers us the Jesus who is there to help, because he's one of us, and has trodden the path before us. It offers us the Jesus who has inaugurated the new covenant, bringing to its fulfilment the age-old plan of God. And it offers us, above all, Jesus the final sacrifice; the one who has done for us what we could not do for ourselves, who has lived our life and died our death, and now ever lives to make intercession for us. We come to the Eucharist because we want this Jesus: 'Let us therefore approach the throne of grace with boldness, so that we may receive mercy and find grace to help in time of need.' And we go out gladly to follow this Jesus wherever he leads: 'let us run with perseverance the race that is set before us, looking to Jesus, the pioneer and perfecter of our faith'.

CHAPTER TWO

The Battle Won: Colossians

It was already nearly sunset when we reached the place. There were no signs to say we were there, but the spot was just as we'd been told. To the south, mountains going steeply up to eight and a half thousand feet, with ice-cold water cascading down. Just along from us, the river which those torrents joined. And here, in front of us, a mound of earth maybe fifty feet high, stretching back over several acres. We scrambled up, and stood on the top. And there, with the sun going down, and the music of the river in our ears, we read aloud words that were first heard on that spot, words that declare that the great battle has been won:

He is the image of the invisible God,
   The firstborn of all creation;
For in him all things were created
   In heaven and on earth:
Things visible and things invisible,
   Whether thrones or dominions,
   Whether rulers or powers –
All things were created through him and for him.

He is before all things,
   And in him all things hold together;
And he himself is the head
   Of the body, which is the church.

He is the beginning
   The firstborn from the dead,
   So that in everything he might be pre-eminent.
For in him all God's fullness was pleased to dwell,

And through him to reconcile all things to himself,
  Whether things on earth or things in heaven,
Making peace through his blood, shed on the cross.

                                   (Colossians 1.15–20)

Colosse is inland from Ephesus; put crudely, it's about half-way down Turkey on the left, and in a bit. It was destroyed by an earthquake in about 64 AD; it silted up, and it's never been either rebuilt or excavated, unlike its neighbours Laodicea, about eleven miles away, and Hierapolis, four miles further again. (Hierapolis is the modern Pammukele, where the hot springs are, which you see on the TV advertisements done by the Turkish tourist board. By the time the cold water of Colosse and the hot water of Hierapolis reach Laodicea, they are both lukewarm, which explains Revelation 3.14–20; but that's another story for another day.) For that little town Colosse, and the tiny group of Christians within it, Paul wrote from prison a stunning short letter, in which the victory of Christ over the powers becomes a central and vital theme.

But what are these 'powers'? And in what does the victory consist? And how does knowing about it help us in following Jesus today?

Paul's readers – or rather hearers, since his letters were designed to be read out aloud in the little church – would have had no difficulty in answering the first of these questions. They lived in a world of 'powers'. The great historian Robin Lane Fox, writing about pagan beliefs of this time (and using evidence from Hierapolis among other places), points out that when things went wrong, people didn't blame each other:

They named supernatural culprits, and traced their actions to enmities in heaven. Artemis was hostile to Pan, Earth to Apollo, virgin Athena to loving Aphrodite . . . Because the gods were 'present' and manifest, it was necessary to ask them about [things] which might concern them. Otherwise, they might be 'unpropitious' . . . The old compound of awe and intimacy was still alive. (*Pagans and Christians*, Penguin, 1988, pp. 236–7)

Ancient pagans, like some animists to this day, thought of the world as peopled with hostile, or potentially hostile, forces. If you were going on a sea voyage, you had better propitiate the sea-god first. If you were fighting a war, you needed Mars on your side. If you were in love, you had better make sure you'd got the help of Aphrodite. And so on. And so on. In fact there were so many 'and so on's that life became extremely complicated, and not a little threatening. And a lot of ordinary folk went about their daily business in a climate of fear and uncertainty. They did their best to stay out of trouble; but often the best wasn't good enough, and the demons that lurked behind every bush would get you anyway.

As often as not, the gods and demons would act through human agency. If Rome won a victory over Britain, that was because the goddess Roma was stronger than the goddess Britannia. The earthly battlefield and the heavenly battlefield were not separated by a great gulf; the heavenly was the hidden dimension of the earthly, the extra feature of ordinary reality that explained what was 'really' going on. The principalities and powers were not far away. They were the inner dimension of exterior events.

Do we smile at this stuff? If we do, we are smiling at our own face in a mirror. Who runs *our* world? The politicians? Forget it. They profess themselves helpless; they are the victims of 'forces' beyond their control. They try to take the credit when things go well, but when things go badly the truth comes out. It's all a matter of economic forces. *Forces*? I see no forces. But they must be pretty powerful. They've kept us in recession these last three or four years. They create floods of refugees, and the most powerful people in the world can't sort them out. They have thrown millions of people out of work. They have pushed thousands of businesses into bankruptcy. Walk through our big cities today, and in one shop doorway after another you'll see young homeless people, begging. Who put them there? Ask any politician; ask any economist: it was economic forces, they'll say. It was the political climate. It was the world economic situation.

Look wider. Why have we not solved the problem of Bosnia, or of Rwanda, or of Northern Ireland? We have spy satellites that tell us everything we could possibly want to know about the world. We have departments of politics and economics in universities all over the place. We have computers that can tell you anything about anything. But we can't stop people shelling each other to bits in the snow, or driving each other from their homelands with machetes. Why not? Political powers. The post-Cold War climate. Tribal allegiances. And if we ask why it is that this planet is perfectly capable of growing enough food and distributing it to every man, woman and child who breathes, and yet millions of them are starving, the answer is the same. There are *forces* which stop us doing it.

That's the language we ourselves use. We can't touch and see these forces. Some of them may, for a while, come to be quite closely identified with certain human beings; but take that person away, and the force will still remain. As is often said, it isn't the managing director who runs Ford Motor Company; it's Ford Motor Company that runs the managing director.

Force; power; climate; entities bigger than the sum total of the human beings involved. A set of situations that nobody wants but nobody can do anything about. The only significant difference between us and our pagan ancestors appears to be that they recognized the situation and gave the forces vivid names, while we hide them behind the grey obscurity of vague words, in order to go on flattering ourselves that, as the Mastercard advertisement says, 'You've Got the Whole World in Your Hands.' Which is, of course, what the serpent promised Eve: you will be like gods, knowing credit and debit.

So maybe we need, and need rather badly, to go back to the foot of Mount Cadmus, and stand by the river Lycus, and hear what the Colossians heard. What did Paul want to get across to them above all?

The letter to the Colossians is all about saying 'thank you'. Paul begins by thanking God that there is a church in Colosse at all (1.3). His prayer for them focuses on their being able to give thanks to the Father (1.12). The central section of the letter begins with thanksgiving (2.7); and, when Paul sums up the whole long argument, this is how it concludes: 'whatever you do, in word or deed, do everything in the name of the Lord Jesus, giving thanks to God the Father through him' (3.17). Gratitude is the name of the game (4.2).

And what are they to give thanks for, above all? That God *has rescued them from the power of darkness, and has transferred them into the kingdom of his beloved son*, in whom we have redemption, the forgiveness of sins (1.13–14). That is Exodus language. Just as the children of Israel were brought out of slavery under Pharaoh and were established as God's free people, so now, by the preaching of the gospel, people everywhere can be transferred from the grip of the powers into the kingdom of Jesus – *because* he is the image of the invisible God, the firstborn of all creation. Events in the sociopolitical world carry an interior meaning, and often a threatening or disturbing one; the events of Jesus of Nazareth, his life, his death and his resurrection, carry an interior meaning, a powerful and liberating one. He is the image of the invisible God. And this God made the world, loves the world, is in the business of rescuing the world, and calls us to follow his Son as rescued rescuers.

So where do the 'powers' come in? Paul has three things to say about them in this letter.

First, in the great poem which I quoted a moment ago (1.15–20), we find the vital starting-point. *All things were made in Christ, through Christ and for Christ.* All things – including the 'powers'! The world is not ultimately divided into bits that are irreducibly good and bits that are irreducibly bad. Everything – the invisible things as well as the visible – was made by the creator, through the agency of his eternal Son, whom we know as the man Jesus. God intended his world to be ordered, not random; to be structured, not chaotic. He intended what came to be called the powers, the forces, to be part of the way his world worked. That is where we must start.

What went wrong, then? Why are the powers so threatening? What went wrong was that human beings gave up their responsibility for God's world, and handed their power over to the powers. When humans refuse to use God's gift of sexuality responsibly, they are handing over their power to Aphrodite, and she will take control. When humans refuse to use God's gift of money responsibly, they are handing over their power to Mammon, and he will take control. And so on. And when the powers take over, human beings get crushed. (Conversely, when you see human beings getting crushed, it's usually because there are powers at work that humans are powerless to stop.)

So the second point that Paul makes in the logical sequence is the one which comes midway through the second chapter. For most of chapter 2 he is urging the Colossians that, since they are in Christ, they don't need to submit any longer to the 'powers'. He has in mind especially the 'powers' or forces that control the different nations and races of the world, and that will try to squeeze the members of the young Church into their own categories and philosophies. Now see what Paul does. He goes back to the event of the cross. Why was Jesus crucified? What was the 'meaning', the 'inside', of this event? To anyone in the ancient world, the question answers itself, as it might do today. Why did so many people die in Sarajevo? Why did people die in Tiananmen Square? Why, why did so many die in Rwanda? Same answer: they got in the way of forces, of powers.

Jesus took on the principalities and powers. He lived, and taught, a way of being Israel, a way of being human, which challenged the powers at every point. The powers said you should live for money. Jesus said you can't serve God and Mammon. The powers said that Israel's path to liberation would come through the sword. Jesus said that those who take the sword will perish by the sword. The powers said that Caesar was Lord of the world. Jesus proclaimed the kingdom of God.

What happens to people who stand up to the powers? It looks fine for a while; and then the tanks roll in. Anyone looking at the crucified Jesus would draw the conclusion that that's what had happened. The powers killed him; that's what they do to people who challenge them. The powers nailed up above his head the charge of which he was guilty: he was a rebel. They stripped him naked and publicly humiliated him. They celebrated their triumph over him. Nobody stands up to us like that, they said, and gets away with it. You can't beat the system.

Now listen to Colossians 2.13–15, and see how Paul stands all this on its head:

> When you were dead in your sins, and in your physical uncircumcision, God made you alive together with Christ. He forgave us all our sins, because he blotted out the record of our legal offences: in fact, he nailed it to the cross. *He* stripped the powers and authorities naked; *he* made a public example of *them*; *he* celebrated his triumph over *them*!

Here is the great irony that stands at the heart of Colossians. This is the reason why the Church has to learn gratitude. The cross was not the defeat of *Christ* at the hands of the *powers*; it was the defeat of the powers at the hands – yes, the bleeding hands – of Christ. This is the great theme of Passiontide: 'the royal banners forward go'.

Do you remember that scene in *Jesus Christ Superstar*, when Jesus and the disciples are approaching Jerusalem? Simon the Zealot urges Jesus to go ahead and become king in worldly terms. Jesus, he says, will get all the power and the glory. Jesus, in reply, quietly and sadly tells Simon that neither he, nor any of the other players in the game, have any idea what power and glory really are. And he goes on his way, the way of the cross, the way which totally subverts all the earthly powers. The power of the bleeding love of God is stronger than the power of Caesar, of the law, of Mars, Mammon, Aphrodite and the rest. That is the point that Paul grasped. And that is the reason for the Colossians' gratitude. The battle has been won.

And so the third point that Paul makes about the powers, astonishingly, is that they have been *reconciled* to Christ. Having been defeated, they are not annihilated. God is in Christ making a new world; now, however, brought into new order under the authority of Christ. Colossians 1.20 (in parallel to 1.16) says that through him God reconciled to himself all things, things in earth and things in heaven, making peace through his blood shed on the cross. To say that you must not worship Aphrodite is not to say that you must become sexless beings. To say you can't serve God and Mammon doesn't mean we should give up using money. To say that racial *prejudice* is wrong doesn't mean we can't celebrate the *differences* between us. God intends the powers to serve him, and to serve and sustain his human creatures.

Let's sum up where we've got to. The powers were created good, but got too big for their boots because we humans allowed them to. On the cross, Christ has defeated these rebel powers, and stripped them of their ultimate power. Now he seeks to reconcile them, to create a new world, ordered by the power of the love of God. That is the context in which the Colossians have now been set free – free from the powers, free to follow Jesus.

That is why Paul now urges them to thanksgiving, and to what we might call thanks*living*. He wants them so to understand what the true God has achieved for them in Christ that they will praise him from the bottom of their hearts (1.12–23). He wants them so to understand that they are in Christ, and that therefore no other philosophy or system has any claim on them, that they will celebrate their having died to the old world and come alive to the new (2.6—3.4). He wants them so to grasp the truth of this new way of being human that they will live their lives on the basis of that gratitude, and so be able to put to death all the bits and pieces of the old way of life, and to discover the joy of the new way (3.5-17). In the third chapter of the letter Paul sets out a bracing ethical programme of living in Christ, of following Jesus: no sexual immorality; no anger and violence. But that programme does not stand by itself. If you try and live that way without recognizing the defeat of the powers, you will fail. The ethical programme stands foursquare on the victory of the cross. The powers of lust, that tell you you can't resist them; the powers of fear, suspicion and greed, that tell you you must get angry and use violence – these powers were defeated on the cross. They have no rights over you. The battle has been won.

Paul's vision of the Christian life is thus (as has often been pointed out) of a life lived between D-Day and VE-Day. The decisive battle has been won; the battles we face today are part of the mopping-up operation to implement that victory. We are called to thanks*giving*, where we stand at last in the truly human relationship to the creator and the world; and we are called to thanks*living*, where we behave as the free subjects of the true king, and owe the powers nothing at all. There is now only one Power we are to follow, and that Power has a human face, a face once crowned with thorns.

How can we celebrate and put into practice this victory today? How can we follow this Jesus into genuine victory? It is surprisingly simple. Every time you kneel down to pray, especially when you pray the prayer of the kingdom (which we call the Lord's Prayer), you are saying that Jesus is Lord and that the 'powers' aren't. Every time you say grace at a meal you are saying that Jesus is Lord, and that the world and all it offers is his, and has no independent authority. And every time we celebrate the Eucharist, we celebrate the victory of Jesus Christ in a way which, by the power of its symbolic action, resonates out, into the city, into the country, into the world, into our homes, into our marriages, into our bank accounts – resonates out with the powerful message that God is God, that Jesus is his visible image, and that this God has defeated the powers of evil that still enslave and crush human beings today. 'Eucharist' means 'thanksgiving'; thanksgiving for the work of Christ is the most powerful thing we can ever do. The task of the Church is to get on with implementing the victory of the cross; and if we grasped that vision and lived by it, we would be able at last to address some of the problems in the Church and the world that loom so large and seem so intractable. The battle has been won; let's get on and implement it. Let us follow our victorious Lord wherever he goes.

I brought away a few little stones as souvenirs from my visit to Colosse. I hope they will excavate the site soon, so that we can see if it tells us anything more about the early church who first heard this wonderful letter. But I hope even more that this chapter will stimulate people to excavate this letter and discover some of its hidden treasures for themselves. We have just scratched the surface here; but we have seen enough to help us continue on our way with gratitude. The battle has been won; let's celebrate it, by following the Lord who won it.

CHAPTER THREE

The Kingdom of the Son of Man: Matthew

If you've ever wondered why the New Testament is the book most often bought and least often read in our culture, you'll find the answer on the very first page:

> Abraham begat Isaac begat Jacob begat Judah begat Perez begat Hezron begat Aram begat Aminadab . . .

How much of this can you stand? I don't mean the exhausting thought of all that begetting; I mean the sheer literary nightmare of being hit in the face by a family tree at the very start of the book. A lot of folk pack it in right there. Let's face it: other people's family trees are about as interesting as other people's holiday videos.

Unless, just possibly, the line went on like this: Nahshon; Salmon; Boaz; Obed; Jesse . . . and David. Now we're getting somewhere. Royal family family trees tend to be just a little bit more juicy. They're worth remembering. In fact, this one is already quite juicy; Matthew has reminded the reader of at least two snippets the pious Jew might have wanted to forget. This family tree includes some women; not the obvious ones like Sarah and Rebecca and Rachel, but the dubious ones like Tamar (who seduced her father-in-law), Ruth (the foreigner), and, just coming up, Bathsheba – whose name echoes down the annals of shame all the way to Thomas Hardy. (Of course, let me hasten to add, in each case any shame there is properly belongs to the men involved.) And at this point the reader who likes to be teased into thought begins to realize why the first page of the New Testament, although undoubtedly the most boring page for the casual browser, is packed with a charge so potent, underneath that bland exterior of continual begetting, that when it finally explodes you can hear it for miles around.

Do you know what that first page of Matthew's gospel reminds me of? You may know Handel's great Coronation Anthem, *Zadok the Priest*. Think of how it starts. You have a sequence of broken chords; harmless enough, a few little variations. At one point we think it's going to grow and swell into something important, but it turns away and goes on with its broken chords, this way and that, including some in a minor key. But then, little by little, we sense that it really is going somewhere; it grows, and grows again, and the harmony works back to where it should be, and, when the swell and the surge is about to become unbearable, the whole thing explodes as the choir crashes in:

Zadok the Priest – and Nathan the Prophet – ANOINTED SOLOMON KING . . .

That, I suggest, is precisely the effect that Matthew's prologue is intended to have on a reader whose ears are attuned to hear his music. Abraham . . . David; ah, we're getting somewhere? No, we seem to be going back to the arpeggios: Solomon, Rehoboam, Abijah . . . and then, to our alarm, it goes into the minor key for a moment: Josiah, Jechoniah, and off they go to exile in Babylon! What's *that* doing in a family tree? Well, wait a moment; back comes the rhythm, the broken chords – and now, yes, it's building up at last: Zadok (not the same one as in the anthem, of course), Achim, Eliud, Eleazar, Matthan, Jacob, and then at last Joseph, the husband of Mary, *of whom was born Jesus, who is called Messiah, King of the Jews*. Matthew's whole gospel is, in fact, a Coronation Anthem. And the only sensible reason for going to church and hearing Matthew read is so that we can learn how to join in.

But who is being crowned King? Matthew gives him two names, and explains them both. He is to be called 'Jesus', which means 'YHWH saves' – because, says Matthew (1.21), he will save his people from their sins. That is, he will deliver his people from their exile, which was the punishment for their sin. He will be the King who will go down into exile with his people and lead them up and out the other side. And the real exile is not the Babylonian one. It is the satanic exile of sin and death.

The second name is 'Emmanuel', which means 'God with us' (1.23). Matthew has drawn together the two threads of Jewish expectation. First, God will save his people from their sins; yes, and he'll do it through the King, Jesus. Second, God himself will come and dwell with his people. Yes, says Matthew; he'll do that, too, through the King, Jesus. This book celebrates the coronation of the saviour, the God-with-us King.

Turn to the end of the gospel and you'll see how it's all worked out. The disciples come to the risen Jesus on the mountain in Galilee. And what does he say to them?

> All authority in heaven and on earth has been given to me; so go and make disciples of all nations, baptizing them . . . and teaching them . . .; and look, *I am with you always*, even to the close of the age. (28.18–20)

Do you see how Matthew has tied his gospel together with the Emmanuel theme? Jesus is to be called Emmanuel, God with us; now, he says, *I* am with you always. And the one who says it is the one who has died on the charge of being the King of the Jews, and who has been raised again. In other words, he is the one who has saved his people from their sins. The Coronation Anthem ends with the same chord with which it began.

Now if this was all we had to say about Matthew, we would already know that we were faced with a book of great power, summoning us to a fresh allegiance to our sovereign and saving Jesus, our Emmanuel. To this extent, the book already functions as a call to worship, and to follow. We cannot simply mouth the name Jesus without thinking; we are speaking of the King, the Emmanuel, the one who has promised to be with us always. But Matthew's gospel, of course, goes further, and hooks into the theme we were studying in the previous chapter on Colossians. This is the story of how evil has been defeated; and it is told in such a way as to invite us to share in the fruits of victory. Matthew, too, is calling his readers to follow Jesus.

Take that little phrase in Jesus' last speech at the end of the book: 'All authority in heaven and on earth has been given to me.' That is a fairly clear reference to a bit of the Old Testament which is of the greatest possible significance for Jesus and early Christianity, but which is regularly misunderstood by Christians today. Let us pause for a moment, and think about the seventh chapter of the book of Daniel.

If this were a Sunday school class, I could ask the front row what they know about Daniel; if there was an answer, I suspect it would have something to do with lions. In chapter 6 Daniel gets thrown into the lion's den. And to everybody's surprise, *nothing happens*. (Actually, I suspect the lions were as surprised as anybody; you can almost imagine a cartoon, with balloons coming out of each puzzled lion's head, saying, 'Thinks: Why aren't we eating this chap?') In the morning, along comes the king, and looks down into the pit; when he finds Daniel safe and sound, he brings him out; and he makes a proclamation that everyone should worship the god of Daniel, because he is the living God, and his kingdom (note that) – his kingdom will last for ever.

At this point the book of Daniel suddenly changes gear, and instead of lions we have monsters. Daniel has a dream about fabulous, ghastly monsters – a winged lion, a bear with tusks, a four-headed leopard, and a huge monster with ten horns; if you made a video of this it would carry at least a '15' sticker, quite possibly an '18'. And these monsters, especially the last, are making war on the people of God (7.21). But then, as in the lion's den, the King comes and takes his throne; and the human figure, who represents the people of God in the language of the dream, is lifted up on the clouds, and seated next to the King, the Ancient of Days. To this one, this human figure, this 'one like a son of man', is given the kingdom which shall last for ever. *The kingdom of God is shared with the Son of Man.* This is Daniel's version of the Coronation Anthem. God will save his people, here represented by this 'son of man', from their exile, from their oppression at the hands of the monsters, the pagan nations. He will save his people from their sins, and will give them a kingdom which shall never be destroyed. All authority in heaven and on earth will be given to them, that is, to this 'son of man' who represents them.

Perhaps you can now see that this combination of themes is precisely what Matthew has chosen as the framework for his gospel. He brings before us, in his great Coronation Anthem, one who will save his people from their sins; and one who, precisely in doing so, will share the very throne of God; one who is 'God with us', God representing us, God alongside us, God with us always, even to the end of the age. The 'coming of the Son of Man on the clouds' (as in Matthew 24.30; 26.64) is not the *return* of Jesus at some point in the future. It is his vindication, his victory,

his bursting from the spicèd tomb,
his riding up the heavenly way.

The book of Daniel gives us this amazing video script about the coronation of the 'son of man' – his suffering the pain of God's people, and his subsequent vindication. Matthew has taken this script and has cast Jesus in the title role. He has written a gospel, a Coronation Anthem, all about the kingdom of the Son of Man. And he is steadily, throughout his gospel, inviting his readers to follow this King, this Son of Man, this Jesus.

Now at last we can understand the fascinating passage which comes at the centre of the gospel (Matthew 16.13–28). 'Who are people saying that the Son of Man is?' asks Jesus. 'Oh – John the Baptist; Elijah; Jeremiah; one of the prophets,' reply the disciples. Jesus was perceived as a prophet, warning Israel of her impending doom unless she repented pretty quickly. The monsters were closing in around the people of God, coming in for the kill. 'But you,' says Jesus, 'who do you say that I am?' And Peter replies: 'You are the Messiah, the Son of the living God' (16.16). Jesus accepts the title. He is the true King, as yet uncrowned. The disciples have now caught up with the first part of the family tree. This is the story of the son of Abraham who is the true son of David.

But Jesus at once moves them on, hurries them forward, to the second part of the family tree. 'From that time on, he began to show them that he had to go to Jerusalem, suffer at the hands of the elders, and be killed, and on the third day be raised' (16.21). Peter couldn't get hold of that; but Matthew expects his readers to grasp the point. The son of Abraham who is the son of David is the one who will save his people from their sins. He is the one who will undo the great exile, the great Babylonian captivity of the people of God. Since, as we have seen, one of the controlling images for that great act of liberation is Daniel's picture of the 'son of man' being surrounded by the man-eating monsters and then, astonishingly, being rescued, vindicated and enthroned, Jesus at once goes on to issue the command to follow him:

If you want to come after me, deny yourself, take up your cross, and follow me; follow me right into the lion's den; for the Son of Man will come in the glory of the Father, and then he will repay everyone for what has been done. Truly, i say to you, there are some standing here who will not taste death before they see the Son of Man coming in his kingdom. (Matthew 16.27–8, expanded)

There are some of Jesus' hearers, in other words, who will live to sing the Coronation Anthem themselves. The kingdom of the Son of Man; the son of David who will save his people from their sins; the Emmanuel who will share the glory of the Father; all is to be revealed within a generation, and Jesus' hearers are to follow him and discover it all for themselves. What could Matthew possibly mean?

He quite clearly regards this prophecy as fulfilled by the time the risen Jesus stands before the disciples in Galilee. All authority, Jesus says, *has been given to me*; the Daniel prophecy has come true. What has happened between Matthew 16 and Matthew 28? Jesus has been crucified and raised from the dead.

This, then, is Matthew's interpretation of the Passion of Jesus. When we think of the cross, our minds are so filled with different images that the whole thing goes fuzzy. Matthew gives us a set of lenses through which we can bring it sharply into focus. The cross is the decisive *royal* act; Jesus on the cross is Jesus the son of David, the King of the Jews. That's the first lens. The cross is the decisive *saving* act; this is how he is saving his people from their sins. That's the second lens. The cross is the moment when the monsters finally close in on the Son of Man; the forces of evil vent their wrath on him, pour it all out until there is none left. The cross is the *defeat of evil*. That's the third lens. But the cross is also the work of the Emmanuel, God-with-us; and it is therefore also the victory, the victory in which the Son of Man bears the saving purposes of the Father through his atoning death and out into the new day of the resurrection. The cross is the great *divine* act; that's the fourth lens.

The cross and the resurrection thus establish the kingdom of the Son of Man. That is, they achieve the purpose for which God called Abraham in the first place, the purpose for which God called David to be the man after his own heart, the purpose which seemed to be thwarted by the exile but which was actually thereby designed to come to its great climax. Here Matthew stands shoulder to shoulder with Colossians, which we looked at in the previous chapter. The powers, the great monsters, seemed to be winning the victory; but the cross and resurrection show that all authority has now been committed to Jesus.

Where does this leave us? Matthew, of all the gospels, makes this crystal clear. If the Son of Man is the King of the world, we who worship him are to follow him, and are therefore sent into the world with a great commission. We are to make disciples, learners, followers; we are to baptize them, and teach them to observe all that Jesus commanded. There is no corner of the created universe over which Jesus does not claim rightful sovereignty. We are to be his agents, his ambassadors, in bringing the word of his kingdom to all his subjects. The Coronation Anthem contains a line of music for every creature, and the harmony will not be complete until they all join in.

But what are all these things which Jesus commanded his followers to observe? You may have noticed that I have managed to write about Matthew for several pages without mentioning the Sermon on the Mount (Matthew 5—7); which is rather like talking about modern American films without mentioning Woody Allen. But the Sermon on the Mount fits like a glove into the themes we have been looking at. (As do the other four discourses which together make up Matthew's great five books, the new Pentateuch, the books of the new covenant: chapters 5—7; 10; 13; 18; 23—5.) And the teaching of that Sermon is of course the subversive message that the meek shall inherit the earth, and that the peacemakers will be called the children of God.

And where does that bite today? Was I the only person in Britain who found it heavily ironic that on the same news bulletin, in the spring of 1994, we were told that, despite requests from our own general for more peacemaking and peacekeeping troops in Bosnia, we were unable to supply them, *and* at the same time that the financial interests of this country dictated that we should supply weapons to people in other parts of the world, with which to blow one another to smithereens, even if it means doing shady deals which broke the government's own guidelines? Completely comprehensible, of course, in terms of complex contemporary politics. But with Matthew's Coronation Anthem open in front of us, we cannot close our ears to the call of Jesus. What will it profit us if we gain the whole world and lose our own true identity? Even if we were to win all the arms contracts in the world, and were thereby to attain full employment and great prosperity, would we be proud to think that wherever people were killing each other they were doing so with weapons labelled 'made in Britain'? Is that what this country is all about? How can we condemn Baruch Goldstein, who killed fifty Arabs at prayer in a mosque, while we run an economy that depends on people doing that fifty times over every week? Which king are we following, anyway?

In the kingdom of the Son of Man, the power that counts is the power of love. It is the rule of Emmanuel, God-with-us. And if we celebrate that fact, as we do supremely in the Eucharist, let us heed the call that goes with it: that we should go into the world to follow this Emmanuel, to work and pray so that the healing celebration of the Coronation Anthem may woo this weary old world back to the God who made it and who loves it still. 'May the King live for ever! Alleluia, Amen.'

CHAPTER FOUR

The Glory of God: John

And the Word became flesh, and dwelt among us; we beheld his glory, glory as of the only-begotten of the Father, full of grace and truth (John 1.14). It echoes through our churches at Christmas time. It echoes down the corridors of memory: our own memory of Christmasses long gone, the collective memory of the Church, the subconscious memory of the human race. *In the beginning was the Word . . . and the Word became flesh.* Christmas Carol services have made John's prologue one of the most famous of Bible passages. But the words about the Word are not just about Christmas. They reach out with the rich message of Jesus, the message that summons us to follow him all the year round.

John's gospel is different. There was a famous conversation earlier this century between Archbishop William Temple and Bishop Charles Gore. Gore said to Temple that he visited St John as one might visit a strange and beautiful foreign country, but that he came home to St Paul. Temple replied that with him it was the other way round. The theologies of Paul and John harmonize at a deep level, but the mood in the two writers is utterly different. As one who cut his teeth on Paul, I have to say I find myself with Charles Gore. I once went for a job interview where I held forth about Paul for some time, and was then asked about John. I said then, and it's still true, that I feel about John like I feel about my wife; I love her very much, but I wouldn't claim to understand her. I didn't get the job.

In style, emphasis, structure – in all the things that make a book what it is – John stands out from the rest. With Paul we are in the seminar room: we are arguing the thing out, looking up references, taking notes, and then being pushed out into the world to preach the gospel to the nations. Matthew takes us into the synagogue, where the people of God are learning to recognize Jesus as their King, their

Emmanuel. Mark, as we shall see, writes a little handbook on discipleship, for the followers of the Servant King. Luke presents Jesus to the cultured Greek world of his day. John, by contrast, takes us up the mountain, and says quietly: 'Look – from here, on a clear day, you can see for ever.' *We beheld his glory, glory as of the Father's only Son.* John does not describe the transfiguration, as the other gospels do; in a sense, John's whole story is about the transfiguration. He invites us to be still and know; to look again into the human face of Jesus of Nazareth, until the awesome knowledge comes over us, wave upon terrifying wave, that we are looking into the human face of the living God. And he leads us on, with our awe and bewilderment reaching its height, to the point where we realize that the face is most recognizable when it wears the crown of thorns. When John says, 'We beheld his glory', he is thinking supremely of the cross. And those who see this glory in this cross are, very shortly afterwards, commissioned to follow the one who has made this glory visible.

I want here to explore three out of the dozens of strands which go to make up this extraordinary tapestry. The first one is all about signposts. John is a canny writer; he gets us to do half the work. In one of the early scenes in the gospel, a passage much beloved of preachers at weddings, he tells the story of the wedding at Cana, and of Jesus changing the water into wine. John's comment, at the end of the story, hooks into the prologue, and at the same time points us forwards into a sequence of signposts. 'This beginning of signs', he writes, 'Jesus did in Cana of Galilee; and *he revealed his glory*; and his disciples believed in him' (2.11). *The Word became flesh, and celebrated a friend's wedding; and we beheld his glory, glory as of one who takes the ordinary and transforms it into the extraordinary.* By saying it's the 'first' sign, John alerts us that there are more to come. And so, at the end of chapter 4, we have the centurion's servant, whom Jesus heals at long distance (4.46–54). John comments that 'this was the second sign that Jesus did'. *The Word became flesh, and healed the sick; we beheld his glory, glory as of the sovereign giver of life.*

Having pointed out these two signs, John now says, in effect: all right, you're on your own from here. He wants us to keep our eyes open, and to keep counting. The next chapter opens with a third sign, the healing of the man at the pool of Bethesda. Chapter 6 begins with the feeding of the 5,000 in the wilderness. Chapter 9 gives us the healing of the man born blind, and chapter 11 tells the story of the raising of Lazarus from the dead. Have you been keeping count? These add up to six signs in the first half of the gospel, which runs from chapter 1 to chapter 12. After that, we move into the upper room, where we have the footwashing scene and the long farewell discourses; and then we come to the crucifixion itself.

What, no more signs? Surely John isn't going to leave us with just six? Anyone who knows about special numbers knows that the number six is nothing compared with the number seven. And why should we have seven in mind? Well, think back to the prologue again. 'In the beginning . . .': John starts off as though he's writing a new Genesis, a new creation story. And so he is. He is talking us through the seven signs of the new creation. What is the seventh sign? The whole movement of the story gives us the answer. The cross is the seventh sign: that is where the glory of God is supremely revealed. John is inviting us to see the mount of Calvary as the mount of transfiguration: *the Word became flesh, and died among us; we beheld his glory, glory as of the one who lays down his life for his friends.*

The 'signs' are the first strand I want you to hold in mind. They lead the eye up to the cross. And they are supported by the second strand, which is a classic example of something you get used to after a while in reading John: he is full of multiple meanings, words and phrases which resonate at different levels. Try this passage:

As Moses lifted up the serpent in the wilderness, even so must the Son of Man be lifted up; that whosoever believes in him may have eternal life. For God so loved the world that he gave his only Son, so that all who believe in him may not perish but have eternal life.

(3.14–16)

What does it mean that the Son of Man must be 'lifted up'? At one level, it clearly refers to the cross. On the cross, Jesus is lifted up above the earth, lifted up in the place of shame, of hard and bitter agony, the place and posture which symbolize a world gone wrong. But at another level this 'lifting up' refers once more to glory; it carries the meaning of 'exaltation' and 'glory'. On the cross, Jesus is lifted up as the true revelation of God, lifted up in the supreme work of love, of gentle and heartfelt compassion, the place and posture which now symbolize the yearning love of the creator for his lost and self-destructive world.

Can we get our minds around the love of God? We can, perhaps, imagine a *creator* God if we try hard enough. We know about making things, and we can guess at the idea of a being who made this world. And we can imagine a *judging* God without too much difficulty. We know about getting cross when things go wrong, and we can guess at the idea of a being whose world rebelled against him and who decided simply to punish it. But try imagining a God who sees his world in rebellion, and loves it so much that he comes in person to take its agony upon himself, and who thereby reveals his true self most fully and gloriously; that's not so easy. The only way you can do it, and can keep the picture in focus, is to understand the cross as the lifting up of Jesus in both senses.

And this 'lifting up' carries a further echo as well. 'As Moses lifted up the serpent in the wilderness . . .' What on earth is that all about? In Numbers chapter 24 the people of Israel sin by grumbling against the Lord; they incur a plague of poisonous serpents, and people are dying from their bites. So God tells Moses to make a bronze serpent and put it on a pole, and anyone who comes and looks at the bronze serpent is healed. It's a strange old story to which John gives a vivid new life. As Jesus is lifted up, the living and dying revelation of the love of God, anyone who looks at him will have life:

> Lord, thy wounds our healing give;
> To thy cross we look, and live.

This same image is used in John 12 to show how the death of Jesus will throw open the gates to the whole world to find new life in this living and dying love. Jesus has arrived in Jerusalem, with the crowds shouting Hosanna. Some Greeks are there for the Passover festival, and they want to see Jesus. Jesus replies:

> 'The hour has come for the Son of Man to be glorified. Truly, truly, I say to you, unless a grain of wheat falls into the earth and dies, it remains alone; but if it dies, it bears much fruit . . .
>
> 'Now my soul is troubled. And what shall I say? "Father, save me from this hour?" No – for this purpose I came to this hour. Father, glorify your name.' Then a voice came from heaven: 'I

have glorified it, and I will glorify it again.' The crowd said that it had thundered. Jesus said, 'This voice came for your sake, not mine. Now is the judgement of this world; now the ruler of this world will be cast out. And I, *when I am lifted up from the earth*, will draw all people to myself.' (12.23–32)

Here is, more or less, the full set of John's imagery about the Passion. The grain of wheat must fall into the earth and die. This is the 'hour' for which Jesus has been waiting: his death is not going to be a sad accident cutting short a promising career, but the climax and purpose of his whole work. In this act God will glorify his name. And, in being thus 'lifted up' – glorified, crucified – Jesus will draw all people to himself. How could it not be so, if indeed his cross is the true revelation of the true God, and if what we see in that revelation is the face of love?

So: the 'signs' point to the new creation through the cross; the 'lifting up' of Jesus insists that the cross itself is the moment of glory, the moment when sovereign love meets a world in agony and grasps that agony to itself. This prepares us for the third theme, which holds it all together.

Strangely, one of the few stories which John has in common with the other gospels he puts near the beginning while the others put it near the end (2.13–22). Jesus comes to the Temple in Jerusalem and drives out the traders with a whip of cords. The Judaeans ask him: 'What sign can you show us for doing this?' and Jesus replies: 'Destroy this temple, and in three days I will raise it up.' They misunderstand him; but John explains that he was speaking of *the temple of his body*.

We must remind ourselves that, for the Jews, the Temple was where the one true God had promised to make his home. The Temple was the place where heaven and earth were joined together. It was the place you went to meet with God. It was the place of sacrifice, of atonement, the place where you went for festivals because you went to celebrate the presence and love of God.

John constantly says and implies that Jesus thought and acted as though he were some kind of replacement for the Temple. When he went up to the festivals, he drew the meaning of the festival on to himself. He does it with Tabernacles in chapter 7. He does it with Hanukkah in chapter 10. And, supremely, he does it with Passover, three times – in chapter 2, chapter 6, and then in chapters 12—19, finally dying as the Passover Lamb, the Lamb of God who takes away the sin of the world. He is the sacrifice, and he is the Temple, just as in chapter 17 he is the great high priest who sanctifies himself so that his people may be presented before God and even joined to God in intimate, loving, family relationship.

This theme, too, was there in the very beginning, in the prologue. In some Jewish writings God's Wisdom was personified as the creator's handmaid, his helper in all that he did. Wisdom looked for a place among human beings where she might dwell; and she chose the Temple in Jerusalem. God the wise creator comes to dwell with his people; he pitches his tent, his 'tabernacle', with them. And the word for 'tabernacle' or 'tent' is the word that John uses when he says, 'The Word became flesh, and *dwelt* among us' (1.14). The Word, the eternal self-expression of God, the one through whom the world was made, pitched his tent in our midst. Only, instead of this taking place in a building, in the Temple in Jerusalem, it took place in a human being. No longer shall we go to Jerusalem, 'to behold the fair beauty of the Lord, and to seek him in his Temple' (Psalm 27.4). All that the Psalms say of the Temple has come true in Jesus. *We beheld his glory, glory as of the only Son of the Father*. The signs point to the great act of the cross, and explain its significance. Jesus' lifting up, or glorification, stresses that the crucifixion is the great revelation of the glory of God, the God of saving and healing love. Now we see why those two things are true. The one who is crucified is the true and living God.

But how can the living God become a human being? How does it make sense? It makes sense precisely in terms of the creation story which John evokes with the very first words of his gospel. The climax of the creation in Genesis was the making of human beings in the image and likeness of God – the great work of the sixth day, bringing creation to its completion. The climax of John's prologue is the incarnation of the Word. Humans were made to reflect God, so that one day God could appropriately become human. And, in case we miss the point, John has that unforgettable scene near the end, when Jesus is on trial before Pilate. Pilate has him flogged, and dresses him up in purple, with a crown of thorns on his head. He brings him out before the crowd, and says, 'Behold – the man!' And by now John's reader knows what this means. *This is the true man, the truly human being*, the one who, crown of thorns and all, truly reflects the image of the loving creator because he *is* the image of the loving creator – the Wisdom of God, the Word of God, the creative self-expression of God. *The Word became flesh, and was crowned king in our midst; we beheld his glory, glory as of the human, bleeding figure, the one given by the Father to save the world.*

And, just as the creation story ended in triumph when God finished on the sixth day all the work he had undertaken, and rested on the seventh day (Genesis 2.1–3), so the last word of Jesus in John's gospel is just that: 'Finished!' (19.30). On the Friday morning, the sixth day of the week, Pilate brought out the man who was God incarnate; on the Friday afternoon God incarnate finished the work he had undertaken. And on the seventh day God incarnate rested in the tomb, rested from his completed labour. *The Word became flesh, and slept among us; we beheld his glory, glory as of the loving God who has finished the work of redemption.*

But like all the New Testament stories, this story isn't only about Jesus. It's about us as well. Jesus is lifted up to draw us all to himself, and to enable us to be for the world what he was for the world. The prologue says that 'To all who received him, who believed in his name, he gave the right to become the children of God' (1.12). Or, again: in 7.38 Jesus says, 'He who believes in me – out of his heart shall flow rivers of living water.' That's the creation image again (Genesis 2.10–14), and the Temple image again (Ezekiel 47.1–12); only now the rivers of living water that flow out of the Temple of God in the new creation come, not just from Jesus, but from all those who believe in him, who follow him, who become in their turn the channels through which his healing love can flow to the world. Therefore the risen Jesus says, in John 20.21: 'As the Father has sent me, so I send you.' And he breathes on the disciples, as God breathed upon Adam and Eve in the beginning, and gives them his own spirit, his own breath of life.

Do you get the point? The whole amazing story of Jesus, with all its multiple levels, is given to us to be our story as we follow him. This is John's ultimate vision of the nature of Christian discipleship. At the end of chapter 21, after Jesus' strange and beautiful conversation with Peter, he issues that haunting summons: don't think about what I may or may not require of the person standing next to you. Your call is simply to follow me. 'If it is my will that he should

remain until I come, what is that to you? You are to follow me'
(21.22). Because of the cross, Jesus offers us, here and now, his own
sonship; his own spirit; his own mission to the world. The love which
he incarnated, by which we are saved, is to become the love which
fills us beyond capacity and flows out to heal the world: so that *the
Word may become flesh* once more, *and dwell* (not just among us,
but) *within us*; having beheld his glory, *we must then reveal his glory,
glory as of the beloved children of the Father, full of grace and truth.*

CHAPTER FIVE

The Servant King: Mark

Two pictures to start with. The first comes from a popular book by the great psychiatrist Carl Jung. He shows a photograph of Adolf Hitler in full rhetorical flight. The caption underneath says: 'This man is going to set all Europe ablaze through his incendiary dreams of world domination.' Fair enough, you think. Then in the text Jung points out that that is what *Hitler* said about *Churchill*. Makes you think, doesn't it?

The second picture is from Mark's gospel, chapter 10. James and John come to Jesus and ask that they may sit, one at his right and the other at his left, when he comes in his kingdom. Jesus explains that sitting at his right or his left is not his to grant; that is for the Father. Fair enough, we think. Then, as we read on, we realize what this means. For Mark, Jesus becomes King when he is crucified, publicly placarded as 'King of the Jews'. And on his right and his left there hang two brigands, two insurrectionists. No wonder Jesus told James and John they didn't know what they were asking for.

What's going on in these two pictures? In both cases, we're faced with what the psychiatrists call 'projection'. I can't face the evil in myself; so I 'project' it out on to somebody else. I accuse them of something that I am worried about because it is lurking deep within my own heart. This, incidentally, is why parents often find their children most irksome when the children most closely reflect the parents; and perhaps this works the other way round as well. We can see quite clearly how projection works in the case of Hitler. As historians of all camps will confirm, it was Hitler himself who had long dreamed of world domination, and who was setting all Europe on fire as a result. But what about James and John?

James and John, by their behaviour all through the gospel story, were eager for Jesus to mount a serious Jewish revolution. Like many other holy revolutionaries of the day, they wanted a Messiah who would defeat the Romans, cleanse the land of paganism, and establish Israel as the top nation in the world. The trouble with that dream was that it always painted its pictures in sharply contrasting goodies-and-baddies, black-and-white tones. One of the Dead Sea Scrolls, reflecting this, calls itself 'The War of the Sons of Light against the Sons of Darkness'.

The Jews of Jesus' day sustained their revolutionary dreams, like many revolutionaries before and since, by painting their oppressors totally evil and themselves totally pure. The problem with that wasn't just that things aren't that simple in real life. The problem was that to think in terms of revolution, of military revolt against Rome, was itself a total betrayal of the purposes for which God called Israel in the first place. Israel had been called to be the light of the world; James and John were bent on extending the darkness, defeating an evil regime with the evil of a violent revolution. God promised Abraham that in his seed all the families of the earth would be blessed; James and John would have been quite content to have had the other families of the earth cursed and reduced to subjection.

When Jesus rebukes them, therefore, it isn't for a minor misunderstanding. It is because they have embraced an entirely wrong vision of God and of his purposes. Instead of sharing Jesus' vision and becoming part of the solution, they had become part of the problem. They were like firemen who had become arsonists.

And so Jesus addresses the twelve with solemn words which point up, for Mark, the significance of the cross, and which point on, for us, to the wider meaning of the cross for us today, not least its clear implications for what following Jesus is all about. He says:

> You know that the kings of the nations dominate them, and their great ones exercise a tyrannous rule over them. That's how it is in the world. But that isn't how it must be with you. Whoever would be great among you, let that person be your servant; and whoever would be your leader, let that person minister to your needs; even as the Son of Man did not come to be served but to serve, and to give his life a ransom for many. (10.42–5)

There is a different sort of kingdom; a different sort of power. The world as a whole runs on the principle that might is right. We like to pretend that we're actually more civilized than that, but again and again, not least in our own century, we have seen that when the chips are down we revert to the same rule: if in doubt, send in the tanks. The trouble is, it sometimes works. It had worked for the Jews in the not-too-distant past; James and John, and thousands of others like them, hoped that it would work for them again. And they were looking to Jesus to spearhead the whole operation (with 'spearhead' being perhaps the operative word).

Now notice: Jesus does not react to this with what we might call the quietist option. To see the full force of this point we need to take a step back for a moment.

When I was in Jerusalem I went, as one does, to the garden of Gethsemane; and among the thoughts which struck me very forcibly in that spot was this. On the night he was betrayed, Jesus could have taken two options very different to the one that he did. He could have summoned the twelve legions of angels, literally or (perhaps) metaphorically: if he'd wanted to spring a surprise attack, there would have been hundreds, maybe thousands, who would have rallied to him. All the Jameses and Johns that were crowding Jerusalem for Passover would have produced swords and daggers from under their cloaks, and they might well have got away with it. They might have established a new regime, a Jewish state free from the Romans, no longer ruled by the jumped-up pseudo-aristocrats who held office as chief priests.

But what would that regime have stood for? Loving your enemies? Praying for your persecutors? Not a chance. It would have been yet one more government that started with high ideals and achieved power by compromising them. Whoever's kingdom that would have been, it wouldn't have been the kingdom of God. Not, at any rate, the God who desired to bless all the nations through Israel.

Jesus' first option, then, was to lead the revolt. The other option was the quietist one, the option of retreat. He could have left Gethsemane, taken his disciples up and over the Mount of Olives, through Bethany and down all the way to the Jordan. King David did it in a single night a thousand years before, fleeing from Absalom. He could have been well away from trouble; they could have set up a community in the wilderness, saying the Lord's Prayer three times a day, and waiting for God to do something. Perfectly safe; apparently pure; probably useless.

Jesus chose neither of these options. Instead, he stayed in Gethsemane, and waited for Judas. Then he stood silent before his
accusers, until, when he spoke, it was with a claim so devastating that
it was bound to secure his immediate condemnation. While the
revolutionaries crucified with him were swearing and cursing, he
stayed largely silent. He did not respond to the mockers, voices outside him and no doubt voices inside him, who told him that the King
of the Jews ought to be defeating the Romans, not dying at their
hands. A crucified Messiah is by definition a failed Messiah. Everyone knew that the Messiah should be the triumphant warrior king.

Everyone, that is, except Jesus; because he had grasped, or rather
been grasped by, a secret – a secret that the Jameses and Johns of this
world, the Adolf Hitlers of this world, never ever glimpse in their
dreams: the secret that there is a different sort of power, a different
sort of Messiah, a different sort of King. The Son of Man came, he
said, to give his life a ransom for many. He was quoting Isaiah chapter 53, the great passage about the Servant of the Lord, who goes like
a lamb to the slaughter, and who was wounded for our transgressions
and bruised for our iniquities. And Mark has written his gospel in
such a way as to make this passage in chapter 10 climactic and
thematic for the whole book. His vision of Jesus is a vision of the
Servant King, who calls his people to follow him.

So if Jesus espoused neither the revolutionary line nor the quietist
position, what precisely was his third option? And what would Mark,
if he were here today, be telling us to concentrate on as we try, in following Jesus, to copy him?

Jesus' third option was to take the projected evil of the world and
to draw it on to himself. You can only understand how that works if
you see the world through Jewish eyes; for the Jews always believed
that their history, their national life, was the focal point of the history
of the whole world. Their God was the creator of the universe;
Jerusalem was the centre of the world; their history was the rudder
that would steer the ship of world history. According to Isaiah, their
sacrificial suffering would be the salvation of the world. And, according to Jesus, that sacrificial suffering would be focused upon one
man, their anointed representative King.

This was the destiny Jesus had glimpsed. He would draw on to
himself the pain of Israel, just as Israel always seemed to draw on to
herself the pain of the world. Instead of projecting evil out on to the

world, instead of keeping the pain in circulation by passing it on, he would bear its full weight in himself. James and John were projecting their own guilt outwards on to the Romans. The Romans were projecting their own imperial insecurities on to their subject peoples. The chief priests were projecting the hollowness of their own system of holiness on to the upstart from Galilee who had symbolically challenged their power base, their whole power system. And when the chief priests handed Jesus over to the Romans, James and John were nowhere to be seen. They had run away, lest perhaps they should after all find themselves sitting on Jesus' right and left as he came into his kingdom.

So what was Jesus doing? An old illustration may help. Do you know how a fox gets rid of its fleas? The fox goes along the hedgerow, and collects little bits of sheep's wool. Then he makes it all into a ball of wool, which he holds in his mouth. Then he goes to the stream, and slowly, slowly, walks down into the water. He lowers himself right down into the water, with the ball of wool in his mouth, until at last he is totally submerged; then he lets go, and the ball of wool floats away downstream, carrying all the fleas with it. The fox emerges, clean.

In this image, Jesus is the ball of wool. The spotless Lamb allows the evil of the whole world to be concentrated on himself. He doesn't keep it in circulation by reacting with violence; nor does he escape into the ineffective innocence of quietism. He takes the weight of the world's evil upon himself, so that the world may emerge, clean.

And Mark's message, the message of the Servant King, the message that you and I have to grasp today, is that we are called to be followers, disciples of this Servant King, so that the victory of the cross may be implemented in the world. 'Disciples' means not just head-learners, not just heart-learners, but life-learners. We have to discover, through prayer, study of the Scriptures, and above all devotion to Jesus himself such as we express when we come to his table, how we in our generation can implement the decisive victory which he won.

Mark's gospel functions as a little manual for Jesus' followers. It is structured very simply in two halves. The first eight chapters introduce us to the first secret: this Jesus of Nazareth is in fact the Messiah. The second eight chapters introduce us to the second secret: this Messiah is not the military warrior, but the Servant King. And at every point, Mark has told the story so as to say to us, his readers: do you get the point? Do you understand? And, if you do, are *you* prepared to follow this Jesus? Are you ready for a life of discipleship? Are you ready to be his agents in implementing the victory which he won?

The Church, ironically, has usually lurched between the two options which Jesus refused in Gethsemane. There have been times when it has been a crusading Church, turning the sword of the gospel into the gospel of the sword, thinking to spread the kingdom of love by the weapons of hatred. God forgive us that we have turned the cross, the great symbol of suffering love, into a symbol which some in the world still have cause to fear. Then there have been times when the Church has withdrawn, has retreated into the private sphere, has thought of its religion as purely a matter between the individual and God, or at best between the Church and God, with nothing to say to the rest of the world. This may sometimes have been a necessary corrective against the crusading arrogance of the first option, but it is not the way of the Servant King. What does Mark have to say?

Mark invites us to stop projecting the guilt and fear we feel inside ourselves out on to the rest of the world. And he invites us to take up our own cross and follow Jesus. He paints a tragi-comic picture of the disciples – blundering about, getting it all wrong, failing to see what Jesus was on about, and letting him down totally. And yet he continues to show Jesus teaching them, loving them, leading them, and ultimately dying for them. That is where we start. If there's anyone reading this who feels that they have blundered about, got it all wrong, misunderstood Jesus and let him down totally, then Mark has good news for them. This good news includes an invitation to Jesus' table, where you can leave the burden behind at the foot of the cross, and receive new life, Jesus' life, to be your new reason for living.

But when we have grasped this, Mark doesn't leave us there. He was probably writing for a church that was undergoing persecution; his invitation to discipleship wasn't a mere matter of private piety, but was a call to people to stand up for the true God, and his Servant Messiah, in the dangerous public arena of the real world. He invites us, in other words, to become part of the solution instead of part of the problem. He invites us to stop being arsonists and to start being firemen.

Mark calls the Church to abandon its imperialistic dreams on the one hand, and its passive non-involvement on the other, and to become for the world what Jesus was for the world. That is what discipleship, following Jesus, really means. That is what is going on when a priest in Walsall has his front door kicked in by the National Front because he has stood up for the rights of the local black population. That is what is going on when Desmond Tutu stands in front of a mob and risks his own life to tell them that violence isn't the answer. That is what is going on when the Church accepts the fact that it suffers in a recession like everyone else, and finds creative ways forward in mission and worship despite losing large chunks of its traditional inherited income. That is what happens when the Church provides a place, and a human presence, where people in pain can come to weep and perhaps to pray. And it is what happens when the Church in a particular country stands up and says 'no' to what is going on in society all around. And if ever there was a time for that, it is right now.

What would it take for the Church in England to embrace this vision of following Jesus? I long to see Christians in this country standing up to the government on the issues of education, of the arms industry, of Third World debt. I long to see the Church standing up to the radical opposition parties on issues like abortion. I long to see the Church lovingly but firmly confronting the media barons who destroy people's lives and reputations for the sake of a sensational story. But it must be done in the right way. We live in a world of Jameses and Johns, of projected guilt and fear and anger. There's no point in the Church simply keeping all of that in circulation. We don't need any more Jameses and Johns, Christians who project their own insecurities out on to the world and call it preaching the gospel. We need – and it's a scary thought – Christians who will do for the world what Jesus was doing.

The Church must be prepared to stand between the warring factions, and, like a boxing referee, risk being knocked out by both simultaneously. The Church must be prepared to act symbolically, like Jesus, to show that there is a different way of living. The Church must be prepared to be the agent of healing even for those, like Aids victims, who are the lepers of modern society. Taking up the cross is not a merely passive operation. It comes about as the Church attempts, in the power of the Spirit, to be for the world what Jesus was for the world – announcing the kingdom, healing the wounds of the world, challenging the power structures that keep anger and pain in circulation. We need to pray that we will have the courage, as a Church and as Christian persons, to follow the Servant King wherever he leads. That, after all, is why we come to his table. We have seen in our century what happens when people dream wild dreams of world domination, and use the normal methods of force and power to implement them. We have not yet seen what might happen if those who worship the Servant King, now enthroned as Lord of the world, were to take him seriously enough to take up our cross and follow him. But that, as Mark reminds us, is precisely what the Servant King calls us to do.

CHAPTER SIX

A World Reborn: Revelation

The communist lecturer paused before summing up. His large audience listened fearfully. 'Therefore,' he said, 'there is no God; Jesus Christ never existed; there is no such thing as a Holy Spirit. The Church is an oppressive institution, and anyway it's out of date. The future belongs to the State; and the State is in the hands of the Party.'

He was about to sit down when an old priest near the front stood up. 'May I say two words?' he asked. (It's three in English, but he was of course speaking Russian.) The lecturer, disdainfully, gave him permission. He turned, looked out over the crowd, and shouted: 'Christ is risen!' Back came the roar of the people: 'He is risen indeed!' They'd been saying it every Easter for a thousand years; why should they stop now?

They weren't just whistling in the dark. The gospel message of Easter is the complete answer to tyranny. And the place in Scripture where that is clearest is that worrying old book at the end, the Revelation of St John the Divine.

The first time I ever read a book of the Bible from end to end it was, oddly enough, the book of Revelation. I was fourteen at the time. The New English Bible had just come out, and I'd been given a copy; and at school there was an hour when we had to read something religious, and I was curious about this strange book at the end of the New Testament. I started it without knowing if it was even readable; I finished it without the question even occurring to me. The funny thing is that I am quite sure I didn't understand what on earth it was all about, but I can still remember the explosive power and beauty of it, the sense that the New Testament I held in my hands had a thunderstorm hidden inside it that nobody had warned me about. I want, in this chapter, to introduce you to this thunderstorm.

Easter is the most thunderous moment in the whole year. Easter is such a huge event that even in the churches we can't cope with it, and we've scaled it down to fit our little minds. The world turns it into fluffy rabbits and chocolate eggs, which are, I suppose, pointing vaguely in the right direction; but they don't really get off the starting blocks. We in the Church have made Easter the source of our present spiritual life: Jesus is alive today, so I can have a personal relationship with him. That's true; it's wonderful; but it is certainly not the full truth of Easter. We have made it the ground of our future hope: Jesus' resurrection proves that there is life beyond the grave. That's true; it's vital; but when you've scaled that little hill you haven't even got to first base camp on the Everest called Easter.

Easter isn't just about you and me and our present spiritual experience, or our hope beyond the grave. Easter is the beginning of God's new world. The idea of a 'New Age', so popular just now, is a feeble pagan parody of the reality, which is this: that when Jesus burst out of the spicèd tomb on the first Easter Day the history of the cosmos changed its course. That's when the real New Age began; and it's perhaps because we've lost sight of that fact that the so-called 'New Age' of today, with all its mumbo-jumbo and its half-baked pseudo-philosophy, has come in to fill the vacuum. Easter is the victory of the creator over all evil. It is the victory of the God of love over all tyranny – tyranny of right as well as of left, and indeed tyranny of the muddled centre that sprouts its ugly head from time to time. It declares that, after all, God is God, and that his kingdom shall come and his will be done on earth as it is in heaven. Easter speaks of a world reborn.

What language can we borrow to do justice to an idea that big? Well, why not try thunder and lightning, earthquakes and tornadoes, devastating terror and joy so rich and full you could swim in it? Yes, we may need the picture-language of the book of Revelation.

Some people have treated this book just as a theological crossword puzzle. But who needs crossword puzzles when you're faced with tyranny and love side by side? The language is strange partly because it's from a different culture. But it's also strange because we in the modern West have made ourselves strangers to thunder and earthquake, to terror and to joy. The closest most of us get to them is in the sanitized little world of television, which we can erase at the touch of a button. If something happens to allow terror or joy to break through and hit us in the face, we can't cope; we go off and have a drink and try to pretend it didn't really happen. But Easter is the time for revolution; if we are in danger of scaling down and domesticating the gospel stories, the Revelation of St John will shake us out of all that, and expose some of our raw nerves to the terror and the joy of the living God.

Revelation begins with a vision of the risen Jesus (1.12–16). Snow-white hair, eyes of fire, feet of polished bronze, voice like a waterfall, and his face like the sun itself – no wonder John fell at his feet as though he was dead. This is where terror and joy meet: this is the Easter Jesus. 'Don't be afraid,' he says; 'I am the first and the last, and the living one. *I died, and look, I am alive for evermore.*' 'And' – and this sounds almost conspiratorial – '*I've got the keys – the keys of Death and Hades*' (1.17–18). Whatever you've lost; whoever you've lost; whatever bits of your life are locked away for sorrow or shame, I've got the keys . . . Tyrants base their power on their ability to kill. Whether it's the invisible tyrant of sin or the visible tyrants that stalk our world still, their power lies in the threat of death. They claim to have the keys of death and hell, but they're lying. Where the tyrants' power runs out, God's power begins. He raises the dead.

This vision of the risen Jesus serves as the magnificent gilded portico into the book. It then has a sort of second introduction, in the form of seven short letters to the seven leading churches in Turkey – Ephesus, Smyrna and the rest. As John knew, they were facing the tyranny of sin within and the tyranny of Rome without, and they were to hold firm to the risen Christ. These letters serve as a corridor, leading us from the portico towards the throne-room, which we reach in chapter 4. John saw a door standing open in heaven; he went through it, in the Spirit, and he saw the living God, with all creation paying him homage. (I shall discuss the meaning of 'heaven' in more detail in chapter 11 below.)

As the vision in the throne-room develops, in chapter 5, something very strange occurs. The one on the throne has a scroll in his hand, and it is sealed; the scroll is the plan of God, the plan of salvation, the divine purpose for recreating the whole cosmos. Somebody has to open the scroll; but nobody can do it. And John says:

I began to weep bitterly, because no one was found worthy to open the scroll or to look into it. Then one of the elders said to me,

'Don't weep. See, the Lion of the tribe of Judah, the Root of David, has conquered, so that he can open the scroll and its seven seals.'

Then [John continues] I saw . . . *a Lamb standing as if it had been slaughtered* . . . (5.4–6)

Here is the Easter message in vivid picture-language. The Lion, the King of Kings and Lord of Lords, has become a Lamb, a sacrificial Lamb, the Paschal Lamb; and by his death he has conquered the powers of evil; so that now the plan of God, God's rescue operation for the whole cosmos, can be unrolled and put into dramatic operation. The strife is o'er, the battle done; now is the victor's triumph won. And the scene concludes with the song of praise being sung by every creature that exists: 'Worthy is the Lamb that was slain, to receive power and riches and wisdom and strength and honour and glory and blessing' (5.12).

Think of Handel's *Messiah* (maybe you just were). Now imagine that whole oratorio as just one of many lines of music, with hundreds of other lines being sung alongside, and all blending together into a huge swelling harmony. And imagine every creature in heaven and on earth – penguins and peacocks, guinea-pigs and gorillas, as well as children, women and men – all singing this extraordinary song. That is how Easter is celebrated in God's dimension of reality. What we Christians do on earth is to add our line to that total harmony. We celebrate together the fact of a world reborn.

But notice the classic *effect* of the Easter message. Do you remember our gospel reading?

Mary stood weeping outside the tomb . . . She turned around and saw Jesus standing there, but she didn't know that it was Jesus . . . Supposing him to be the gardener, she said to him, 'Sir, if you have carried him somewhere, tell me where you have laid him, and I will take him away.' Jesus said to her, 'Mary!' She turned and said to him in Aramaic, 'Rabbouni!' (which means Teacher). (John 20.11–16)

Mary, weeping outside the tomb, stands for all of us. She is weeping bitterly; weeping for herself, yes; weeping for her Lord, yes; but also in her tears weeping for the hope of Israel, cruelly crushed by tyranny; and, in that, for the hope of the world, snuffed out by the power of the world. And Mary weeps on today, in Belfast and Bosnia, in the marshes of southern Iraq and the townships of southern Africa, in the mountains of Tibet and the desert wastes of the Sudan, in the refugee camps and by the rivers filled with bodies; and in the hearts and homes of millions in the West who face tragedies and tyrannies day by day and are without resources to meet them; and in the hearts and lives of Christians who suffer with their Lord here and now.

And on Easter Day Jesus calls Mary by name, and asks, 'Why are you weeping?' He calls us all by name, calls with a voice like the sound of many waters, a voice which goes through the defences that we put up to keep the terror and joy at bay, calls with a voice which we recognize, calls with a love which is stronger than death. And he says to us, too: 'I am the first and the last, and the living one; I died, and behold, I am alive for evermore, and I've got the keys of Death and Hades' (1.17–18). And as the weeping Mary met the living Jesus on Easter Day, so the weeping John discovers that the Lion, who is the Lamb, has conquered; he can open the scroll. And, as the scroll is opened, so the book of Revelation proceeds, in its own amazing picture-language, to work out the cosmic victory of the Lamb over all that is evil, tyrannous and deathly.

After the tears comes the silence:
The slow night, the still sad time,
Rinsed, empty, scoured and sore with salt,
Spent, waiting without hope.
After the night comes the Lamb:
Bright morning star, with living water free
And fresh, the fruit of Friday's toil.

Easter is all about the wiping away of tears. In our fear of terror and joy, we have forgotten the purpose of tears. We have become embarrassed by them – and with good reason, since they are a God-given reminder of the truth which our culture, as much as any communist propaganda, has done its best to make us forget: that we are neither naked apes nor trainee angels, but humans, made in the image of God. Which God? The God who stood and wept at the tomb of his friend; the God who fell down and sobbed in the garden of Gethsemane. We have deemed tears to be child*ish*, whereas in fact they are child*like*; and Jesus told us to be child*like*. We have allowed our proper dislike of emotional*ism* to deceive us into trying to ignore our *emotions*. But if Good Friday and Easter don't stir our emotions, then the tyrant has indeed enslaved us. We have become like a garden paved over with stone slabs. Many people live like that; God help us, many of us even choose it, rather than face the terror and the joy of our own hearts, let alone of Calvary and Easter.

But Easter is all about the garden in which stone slabs are made to look silly. Jesus weeps before Lazarus' tomb; and then he calls him out into life. Jesus weeps again in Gethsemane; then he goes off to confront the tyrant and defeat him. Peter weeps bitterly after he has denied Jesus; and the risen Jesus meets him and loves him and commissions him. Mary weeps before Jesus' tomb; and Jesus meets her, alive. John weeps because the plan of salvation is sealed up, and the world cannot be rescued from tyranny; and his tears turn to worship because of the Lamb who was slain. We can try paving the garden with stone if we like; but come springtime, come Easter, there will be grass pushing its way through. It wasn't, after all, such a silly mistake for Mary to think that Jesus, the true Adam, was the gardener.

But what then is the full hope which Easter unveils? The tumult and battle of the middle chapters of Revelation lead up to the great victory of the Lamb over Babylon, the tyrannous city that has opposed God and his loving purposes. Then, in the last two chapters, we find the vision of the new city which takes the place of the wicked, tyrannous city. It's a vision which makes most ideas of future hope look pretty tame by comparison. It is the Easter vision of a world reborn:

Then I saw a new heaven and a new earth; for the first heaven and the first earth had passed away, and the sea was no more. And I saw the holy city, the new Jerusalem, coming down out of heaven from God, prepared as a bride adorned for her husband. And I heard a loud voice from the throne saying,
'See, the home of God is among mortals.
He will dwell with them as their God;
they will be his peoples,
and God himself will be with them;
he will wipe every tear from their eyes.

Death will be no more;
mourning and crying and pain will be no more,
for the first things have passed away.' (21.1-5)

Most Christians, if pressed, would express their future hope in terms of leaving this world and going to another one, called 'heaven'. But here, at the climactic moment of one of the greatest New Testament books, the heavenly city *comes down to earth*. To be sure, God's people go to heaven when they die; they pass into God's dimension of reality, and we see them no more. But Easter unveils the truth beyond the truth of mere 'survival', beyond the truth even of 'heaven'; the truth that God's kingdom shall come, and his will be done, *on earth as it is in heaven*. Our ultimate destiny is not a disembodied heaven, just as the ultimate destiny of this created world is not to be thrown away, abandoned as secondary or shabby. It's the tyrants who want to blow the world to bits. God wants to re-create it.

The truth of Easter unveils the astonishing fact that the whole world is to be reborn. New heavens and new earth, married together; that is our destiny, that is the world's destiny, and all because of Easter. And the closest we come to this destiny in the present is when, in the Eucharist, we anticipate the heavenly marriage-feast: the symbols of creation, bread and wine, are shot through with heaven, with God's dimension, with the life and love of the Lamb.

And in this new-heaven-and-new-earth there are several things that will have no more place. There will be no barbed wire in the kingdom of God. There will be no bombs or bullets in the kingdom of God. There will be no concentration camps or refugee camps in the kingdom of God. And Revelation has its own list of what won't be there. There will be no Temple; who needs one, when you have the living personal presence of God? There will be no sea; in Revelation, the sea is where evil comes from. There will be no sin, nothing that corrupts and defaces the human reflection of the living God. There will be no death; no mourning; no pain. The tyrant's weapons will all have gone. *And so God will wipe away all tears from all eyes*. Yes, Mary; your tears will be dried. Yes, Peter, yours will be wiped away. Yes, John; your tears are no longer needed, now that the scroll is fully open, the saving plan fully revealed. Jesus' own tears, before Lazarus' tomb and in Gethsemane, are swallowed up in joy. The tears of the Belfast widow will be wiped away. The tears of the Rwandan orphan will be dried. The weeping of the abandoned lover, the bitter tears of the man who's lost his job, the tears of the black child snubbed in the white school, the tears we cry in secret and the tears we cry in our hearts, all will be wiped away.

And it is all because of the Lamb. Here is John's contribution to the biblical picture of cross and resurrection; here is his vision of the Jesus who summons us, in awe and joy, to follow him. Jesus is the one with the eyes of fire and the voice like a waterfall, who died but who is now alive for evermore. Then he is the Lion of Judah, the Messiah who becomes the sacrificial Lamb, who by his blood defeated evil, and rescued human beings and the world from its tyranny. And now, at the end of the story, he is the bridegroom, the one for whom we have longed without knowing it, the one for whom we are made, the one whose love for us is like the sun, and all our earthly loves mere reflecting moons. The wrath of the Lamb, of which Revelation speaks from time to time, is the anger of love against all that hurts and damages the beloved. The *love* of the Lamb is the great reality that undergirds the entire vision.

And it is that love which is revealed at Easter. Without Easter, Calvary was just another political execution of a failed Messiah. Without Easter, the world is trapped between the shoulder-shrug of the cynic, the fantasy of the escapist, and the tanks of the tyrant. Without Easter, there is no reason to suppose that good will triumph over evil, that love will win over hatred, that life will win over death. But with Easter we have hope; because hope depends on love; and love has become human and has died, and is now alive for evermore, and holds the keys of Death and Hades. It is because of him that we know – we don't just hope, we *know* – that God will wipe away all tears from all eyes. And in that knowledge we find ourselves to be Sunday people, called to live in a world of Fridays. In that knowledge we know ourselves to be Easter people, called to minister to a world full of Calvarys. In that knowledge we find that the hand that dries *our* tears passes the cloth on to us, and bids us follow him, to go and dry one another's tears. The Lamb calls us to follow him wherever he goes; into the dark places of the world, the dark places of our own hearts, the places where tears blot out the sunlight, the places where tyrants pave the grass with concrete; and he bids us shine his morning light into the darkness, and share his ministry of wiping away the tears. And as we worship, and adore, and follow the Lamb, we join, already, in the song of Revelation 5.11–14, the song that one day the trees and the mountains and the whales and the waterfalls – the whole world, reborn on Easter morning – will all sing with us:

Worthy is the Lamb that was slain . . .
to receive power and riches and wisdom and strength
and honour and glory and blessing!

To him who sits on the throne and to the Lamb
be blessing and honour and glory and power for ever and ever,
Amen.

PART TWO

A living sacrifice

'I appeal to you therefore, brothers and sisters, by the mercies of
God, to present your bodies as a living sacrifice, holy and acceptable
to God, which is your spiritual worship. Do not be conformed to this
world, but be transformed by the renewing of your minds, so that you
may discern what is the will of God – what is good and acceptable
and perfect.'

Romans 12.1–2

CHAPTER SEVEN

The God Who Raises the Dead

Once upon a time there was a miller who lived in a windmill, and ground flour for the village baker. Day after day the miller used to worry about whether he was producing enough flour. One night, after there had been no wind all day, he hit upon a plan. He would disengage the cogs of the windmill, and work all night turning the machinery himself, by hand. Then he would be sure that there would be enough flour. When morning came, there was plenty of flour, but the miller was slumped asleep on the floor, and the flour never got to the baker. So sound asleep was the miller that he never heard the noise outside, the noise of a rushing mighty wind.

If you have ears, then hear.

What are the implications of the fact that Jesus rose from the dead on the third day after he was executed? We looked at some of them in the last chapter of Part One, focusing finally on the call to follow the Lamb wherever he goes. Now, in introducing our second Part, we look at one of the largest, and hardest, questions of them all, which must be grasped firmly if our following of Jesus is to be rooted as deeply as it needs to be. What does the resurrection of Jesus tell us about the true God? What I want to say divides broadly into three: the surprising command, the sudden crisis, and the surpassing God.

First, the surprising command. The story is told of Moses coming down the mountain to report back to the children of Israel. 'Good news and bad news,' he says. 'The good news is - we've got them down from forty to ten. The bad news is - adultery is still in.' When we think of God giving *commands* to his people, that's the sort of image we naturally go for, isn't it: of a God who has all sorts of rather arbitrary rules, and wants to give us more and more of them, most of them designed, it seems, to stop us doing things we might otherwise want to do. As the college barman in my undergraduate days once said to me, 'The trouble is, everything Jesus is against – I like.'

Now why would one invent a God like that? You may say, We didn't invent him, that's just who God seems to be. Or, perhaps, you are inclined to agree with the critics of Christianity who say that the Church, or perhaps the state, has invented a God like that to keep people under control. There may well be some truth in that; people do invent things to keep others under control. I heard recently of a small boy at a rather strict school who was asked to write down in order the worst things that humans could do, and wrote: Number 1: murder; Number 2: running down the school corridor. We all get things out of proportion.

But this conception of God is in fact a lie. The resurrection of Jesus proves that it's a lie. Do you know what the most frequent command in the Bible turns out to be? What instruction, what order, is given, again and again, by God, by angels, by Jesus, by prophets and apostles? What do you think – 'Be good'? 'Be holy, for I am holy'? Or, negatively, 'Don't sin'? 'Don't be immoral'? No. The most frequent command in the Bible is: *'Don't be afraid.' Don't be afraid. Fear not. Don't be afraid.*

The irony of this surprising command is that, though it's what we all really want to hear, we have as much difficulty, if not more, in obeying this command as any other. We all cherish fear so closely that we find we can't shed it even when we're told to do so. The person who has been worrying all term about exams finally finishes, and still wakes up the next morning with the adrenalin pumping, ready to dash off to the exam room one more time. The person who has worried for years about money, and then suddenly inherits enough and to spare, still finds that they go hot and cold all over when they walk past the bank. It is said that once a practical joker sent telegrams to every member of the then government, saying simply: 'All is discovered – fly at once!'; within twenty-four hours they had all left the country. We are all of us, wrote the anthropologist Nigel Barley, overdrawn at the moral bank. Every one of us has something on her or his mind about which we badly need a voice to say: 'Don't be afraid. It's going to be all right.' As the Lord said to the Lady Julian: 'All shall be well, and all manner of things shall be well.' Let's make no mistake about it: until you learn to live without fear you won't find it easy to follow Jesus.

This surprising command bursts in upon a world in which we eat, sleep and breathe fear. We emerge from the warmth of the womb into the cold of the cosmos, and we're afraid of being alone, of being unloved, of being abandoned. We mix with other children, other teenagers, other young adults, and we're afraid of looking stupid, of being left behind in some race that we all seem to be automatically entered for. We contemplate jobs, and we're afraid both that we mightn't get the one we really want and that if we get it we mightn't be able to do it properly; and that double fear lasts for many people all through their lives. We contemplate marriage, and we're afraid both that we might never find the right person and that if we do marry it may turn out to be a disaster. We consider a career move, and are afraid both of stepping off the ladder and of missing the golden opportunity. We look ahead to retirement, and are afraid both of growing older and more feeble and of dying suddenly.

And these are just the big ones. There are dozens of lesser fears which reinforce and feed on each other. What's more, if we artificially suppress these fears, they pop out in other forms, like phobias. Behind them all looms the fear of death; not, perhaps, for the young, unless they've had a close brush with death for some reason, but certainly a little later.

So you see why this command, 'Don't be afraid,' is one of the hardest of all to keep. Even chastity is reasonably straightforward by comparison. Can you imagine living without fear? I don't mean the sort of secular 'fearlessness' one associates with the heroes of thriller stories or war exploits. There is such a thing as an arrogance, or pushiness, which is simply a cover-up job; I'm not talking about that. I mean, can you imagine living a normal, wise, responsible life *without* the nagging sense that everything is about to go horribly wrong, that you may have made it through the last day, or week, but that this was simply a happy accident, since the universe is basically unfriendly and Murphy's Law will take revenge later or, more likely, sooner? That is how most people live.

To that condition the gospel of Jesus comes with bad news and good news. The good news: there is just one command this time, not even ten. The bad news: this one command tells you not to be afraid, and we haven't a clue how to obey it. We don't like fear, but it's the air we breathe. We don't know any other way to live. This, actually, is why people imagine God as a God who is always giving orders and getting cross with people. We project our fears, yes, and our hatred, up on to the creator of the universe; we call this object, this idol, 'God'; and we are afraid of, and resent, the God we have thus made in our own mirror-image.

And the resurrection of Jesus issues the surprising command: don't be afraid; because the God who made the world is the God who raised Jesus from the dead, and calls you now to follow him. Believing in the resurrection of Jesus isn't just a matter of believing that certain things are true about the physical body of Jesus that had been crucified. These truths are vital and non-negotiable, but they point beyond themselves, to the God who was responsible for them. Believing in this God means believing that it is going to be all right; and this belief is, ultimately, incompatible with fear. As John says in his letter, perfect love casts out fear (1 John 4.18). And the resurrection is the revelation of perfect love, God's perfect love for us, his human creatures. That's why, though we may at any stage in our lives grasp the truth that God raised Jesus from the dead, it takes us all our life long to let that belief soak through and permeate the rest of our thinking, feeling, and worrying lives.

Sometimes this process isn't just a gradual thing; it may involve sudden crises. There's a hidden chapter in the life of St Paul, which is usually ignored by those who see him either as the heroic missionary or the profound theologian, or possibly the misguided misogynist. Acts doesn't mention this hidden chapter, but in our second lesson we heard Paul himself speak of it. At one stage of his work in what he called Asia, and we call Turkey, he says that he went through a horrendous and traumatic experience which seemed to destroy him totally. 'I was so utterly, unbearably crushed', he writes, 'that I despaired of life itself; indeed, I felt as though I had received the sentence of death' (2 Corinthians 1.8–9). And a good part of the second letter to Corinth actually grows out of this experience; the brash, proud Corinthian church had wanted Paul to be a success story, and he had to explain to them that being an apostle, and ultimately being a Christian, was not a matter of being a success story, but of living with human failure – *and* with the God who raises the dead. That's what following Jesus is likely to involve.

The language Paul uses here is the language of depression. Depression is what happens when one particular little clutch of fears get together in a circle, and it forces us to go round and round the circle, worrying about one thing, which leads us to blame ourselves for the next thing, which leads us to be anxious about the third thing, which takes us conveniently back to the start of the circle, and round we go again. And one of the key features of depression is that we put ourselves on trial, produce lots of evidence for the prosecution and none for the defence, find ourselves guilty and pronounce sentence. Paul says, 'I felt as if I had received the sentence of death.' That's exactly what depression is like.

Putting the evidence together, it seems that the component features of Paul's depression were two things. First, he ran into stiff opposition in Ephesus from local folk who didn't like the idea of this new religion, and who did their best to make life difficult for him. That he might have borne; but when he was physically at his lowest ebb (and depression regularly strikes when we are tired, or ill, or physically unfit) he heard that, secondly, one of his largest churches, the Corinthians themselves, had stabbed him in the back by embracing teachers, and teachings, that were leading them away from the truth of the gospel he had taught them.

So had he done it all wrong? Had he failed to teach them properly? Had he failed them, and failed God? Was he going to die under persecution, or in prison, knowing that his work was in ruins, that he'd been called to a unique mission and had just blown it? That, I suggest, was the circle, the treadmill of depression, which struck Paul somewhere in the mid-50s AD.

And, he says, this sudden crisis was to make him rely not on himself but on *the God who raises the dead*. Hadn't Paul been relying on this God before? Hadn't he believed before that God was the God who raises the dead? Of course he had. But somehow there was a new depth, a further, level of his personality which the message of the gospel hadn't fully got through to before. In his Damascus Road experience he had quickly come to see that his life had been based on a mistake. It had been a humbling experience. But even with Paul the humiliation of the gospel took years to get through the different layers of the personality, and in Asia it finally hit a point that it doesn't seem to have reached earlier. He came to the utter end of his own resources; he heard and felt the sentence of death pronounced by the little voice of fear inside; and, he says, 'this was to make me rely on the God who raises the dead'. He had been following Jesus for years; now he realized what precisely it meant to follow the crucified and risen Lord. As a result, he was summoned to stop worrying about his own productivity, and to rely on the rushing mighty wind.

I don't want to give the impression that this new reliance is easy, something that anyone can just do by snapping their fingers and getting on with it. The whole point of what I'm saying is that it isn't like that; that we are so sunk in our habits of fear, and sometimes in the depressions or quasi-depressions which those habits produce, that we find it enormously difficult, and often the work of years and even decades, to hear the gospel of the resurrection with what Sir Edward Elgar called 'our insidest inside'. What I am saying is that the message of the gospel, the message that the true God is the God who raises the dead, can and does go that deep; and that wherever you may be, and whenever you may hit that rock-bottom sense of despair, the gospel can reach you there too. Indeed, that is where it specializes in reaching people. It is when we are weak that we can be strong. When our strength comes to an end, that is when the life-giving wind of God starts to blow with new force.

Therefore, we are not to be surprised if living as Christians brings us to the place where we find we are at the end of our own resources, and that we are called to rely on the God who raises the dead. Living by faith rather than by fear is so odd for us, so scary for us, that it takes a lot of learning. Bit by bit we must open ourselves to the power of this resurrection-God; and sometimes this will only happen when we find ourselves in the sudden crisis where there is nothing else that we can do. Don't be surprised if this happens, not least when you face an uncertain future. Use such an opportunity as the moment when your belief in the resurrection of Jesus, your trust in the God who raises the dead, your determination to follow the Lamb wherever he goes, reaches down one or two levels deeper into your own innermost being, the place where all those fears still live. It's alarming even to confront some of those fears. But until they hear the surprising command, which may only happen in a sudden crisis, they may never be able to turn themselves around from fear to faith.

I hope it's clear by now that the true God is a radically different God from the man-made monster who sits up on a cloud barking out a list of arbitrary commands. We have come back to the beginning of the gospel: either Jesus rose again from the dead or he didn't. If he didn't, then the whole Christian thing is a waste of time; as Paul says elsewhere, if Christ is not raised, let us eat and drink, for tomorrow we die (1 Corinthians 15.32). But if Jesus *did* rise again from the dead, then there is nothing ultimately to be afraid of; as the Psalmist says, the God who has delivered my whole person from death will also deliver my eyes from tears and my feet from falling (Psalm 116.8). It is because Jesus reveals this God to us that we find ourselves called, at the deepest level of our being, to follow him.

All the other commands that enable us to make sense of our human life follow from this one. When we grasp at that which is not ours, it is because we are afraid that if we don't we won't have enough. When we use sex as a means of self-gratification rather than as the glorious affirmation of a lifelong commitment, we do so not just because of lust; lust itself is nurtured in fear, fear of rejection, fear of loneliness. When we lie, we do so because we are afraid that the truth will be embarrassing. And so on. And if we believe in the God who raised Jesus, then, as our fears are dealt with at a deeper and deeper level, as they are met by the astonishing love of the surpassing God, we will be able to leave behind the image of a bossy, bullying God who wants us to keep his laws in order to control us, to lick us into shape, to squash or stifle our humanness or our individuality. Instead, we will be able to follow the true God, the God who raises the dead, in trust rather than fear. The true God gives new life, deeper, richer life, and helps us towards full mature humanness, by prising open the clenched fists of our fears in order to give his own life and love into our empty and waiting hands.

If, then, we recognize the truth about the surpassing God, the God who raises the dead, we can trust him with every lesser task that may come our way. He can be trusted with exams; he can be trusted with jobs, even when they don't necessarily work out the way we thought they should. He can be trusted with marriage, both as we look forward to it with eagerness and trepidation, and when we find ourselves within it and facing the stresses and strains that all contemporary marriages must expect. He can be trusted with money, even when it seems as though there is even less of it available than we had thought. He can be trusted with old age. He can be trusted with death itself. Of course he can; he is the God who raises the dead, who affirms the goodness of human life, who takes precisely the situation where there seems no hope in human terms, and brings new life exactly there.

Our following of the Jesus who reveals this God to us is in line with the vocation of Israel at the end of the exile. Israel, in exile, perceived herself like a childless woman, in a society where that meant great shame; like a divorced woman, without family and without support. Israel was a nation taken over by others, confined to refugee status. This people had faced the sudden and supreme crisis of their whole nationhood. And to them the surpassing God revealed himself afresh, with the surprising command echoing through the prophetic oracles. This is the word of the God who raises the dead, and invites us to follow his risen Son in the new way of life:

> Sing, O barren one who did not bear;
>> burst into song and shout,
>> you who have not been in labor!
> For the children of the desolate woman will be more
>> than the children of her that is married, says the Lord.
> Enlarge the site of your tent . . .;
> do not hold back; lengthen your cords
>> and strengthen your stakes.
> For you will spread out to the right and to the left,
>> and your descendants will possess the nations,
>> and will settle the desolate towns.
>
> Do not fear, for you will not be ashamed;
>> do not be discouraged, for you will not suffer disgrace;
> for you will forget the shame of your youth,
>> and the disgrace of your widowhood you will remember no
>>> more.
> For your Maker is your husband,
>> the Lord of hosts is his name,
> the Holy One of Israel is your Redeemer,
>> the God of the whole earth he is called.
> For the Lord has called you
>> like a wife forsaken and grieved in spirit,
> like the wife of a man's youth when she is cast off,
>> says your God.
> For a brief moment I abandoned you,
>> but with great compassion I will gather you.
> In overflowing wrath for a moment
>> I hid my face from you,
> but with everlasting love I will have compassion on you,

says the Lord, your Redeemer.

This is like the days of Noah to me:
    Just as I swore that the waters of Noah
    would never again go over the earth,
so I have sworn that I will not be angry with you,
    and will not rebuke you.
For the mountains may depart
    and the hills be removed,
but my steadfast love shall not depart from you,
    and my covenant of peace shall not be removed,
    says the Lord, who has compassion on you. (Isaiah 54.1–10)

CHAPTER EIGHT

The Mind Renewed

If it happened today, it would make instant headlines in the *Jerusalem Post*, and perhaps also in the *Washington Post*. 'SYRIAN GENERAL HEALED BY ISRAELI HOLY MAN.' Unthinkable? Yes: that's how it was regarded then as well. Syria and Israel have been slugging it out on and off for three thousand years, and this story is all about a very bemused but very grateful Syrian general discovering that there was a God in Israel who could do things that his local gods apparently couldn't do. His discovery points to the discovery waiting for all who want to follow Jesus: this journey will mean a complete renewal of the mind.

Perhaps you remember the story, which occurs in 2 Kings 5. The great general Naaman was suffering from some incurable skin disease, known loosely as leprosy. He was told that Elisha, the Jewish prophet, would heal him. He hoped for royal treatment: Elisha would surely come out and deal with him as one deals with a great man. What he got was the off-hand style: Elisha sent a message telling him to go and wash seven times in the Jordan. Initially he lost his temper and refused, until his servants made him see sense; he left his pride behind on the bank of the Jordan, and washed, and was cured.

It was at that point that Naaman realized that he had a new problem, and that's where the story really starts. We now have a tale of two muddled men, but muddled in very different ways.

The first of them is this Naaman. A new reality has entered into his life, and we see him struggling to come to terms with it, to put together the bits of the old life into a new pattern so that they will make sense grouped around the new fixed point. This new fixed point is a new belief about God. Up until now he had worshipped his local Syrian god, Rimmon, as a matter of course. But Naaman has now discovered something about Rimmon: he may look fine sitting there in his shrine, but he's not much good when it comes to leprosy. And the bad news is that the enemy, a little way south just over the Golan Heights, worships a god who doesn't have a statue sitting in a shrine, but who beats Rimmon hands down in the healing business. And Naaman recognizes that *this* god has reached out and touched *him*.

He comes back to Elisha and declares: 'Now I know that there is no God in all the earth except in Israel' (5.15). He offers Elisha a present, which is refused; and then he does two things which show his determination to get his thinking straightened out according to the new belief which he has found. First, he works out a way of worshipping this God, even though it's going to be awkward. Second, he faces up to the compromises which he can see he's going to face as soon as he gets back home. First he straightens out his view of God; second, his view of himself.

The first of these is, to us, a little comic. Naaman is still fixated on the idea of territorial gods. Each land has its god. He's discovered that the god who lives in Israel is the really powerful one, so what he does is ask for two mule-loads of Jewish soil, so that even when he's back home he can go on worshipping this god on his own turf. Naaman has not yet worked out the next step in the argument, which is that if the God of Israel is the only true God, he is just as present in Syria as in Israel; but he's on the way. His half-truth is like a glass that is half full, rather than one that is half empty.

His second move is the one I find really fascinating. He says to Elisha, in effect: 'Look, when I get back home, my master, the King of Syria, will expect me to go with him as usual to the house of Rimmon. He's an old man; he leans on my arm; when he bows, I bow. What else can I do? I know it's wrong, but I've got to do it. And I'm sorry.' I am reminded of the ending of T. S. Eliot's poem, *The Journey of the Magi*: the three wise men get to Bethlehem, and they discover that the birth they had come to see meant the death of all that they had been and known up to this point. As a result,

> We returned to our places, these Kingdoms,
> But no longer at ease here, in the old dispensation,
> With an alien people clutching their gods.

That is Naaman to the life. He is caught between the vision of a living, loving and healing God and the reality of his compromised and muddled life, hemmed in by lifeless and useless idols. Paradoxically, when you start to get your thinking about God straightened out, you are bound to run into some muddles as the old, familiar lines of your life are seen from an entirely new angle. Those who have met with the living Jesus, and are trying to follow him, are going to run into just this sort of question.

But was Naaman a compromiser? Shouldn't he have been prepared to say: 'Rimmon be blowed, King of Syria be blowed, I'm going to worship Israel's god and I don't care who knows it'? Shouldn't he have been like Daniel, opening his window towards Jerusalem to pray to Israel's god even when he was in Babylon?

Well, maybe. But it takes a while to learn to be a Daniel. You've got to start somewhere, and Naaman starts with the most important thing of all: to recognize the truth of the muddled situation you're in, to ask for forgiveness where you seem to be compromising, and to take it one step at a time from there. Once again, I think Naaman's glass is half full, not half empty. If Daniel had shrunk back and worshipped the King of Babylon, his would have been half empty; but we'll come to that in a moment.

Where do we fit in to the story of Naaman? One of the reasons people go to church, or read the New Testament, is because they have begun to have a sense that there is no God in all the world but in Jesus. How can you tell? Because there is no other God that loves and heals like this God. There is no other God that says, 'I know you've made a mess of your life, but actually I love you so much that I've dealt with all of that.' There is no other God that takes death and brings out of it new life. The pagan gods and goddesses that our society worships offer you inner peace, but they fail to deliver the goods. There is only one God who loves and forgives and heals, and this God is found, not in one piece of sacred turf, but in Jesus. And once you've glimpsed that, you are going to want to follow him, to worship this God rather than any other, even if we don't understand too much about it all just yet. This is to get the glass half full. This is when we start to put into practice the words of Paul:

> I appeal to you . . ., by the mercies of God, to present your bodies as a living sacrifice, holy and acceptable to God, which is your spiritual worship. Do not be conformed to this world, but be transformed by the renewing of your minds, so that you may discern

what is the will of God – what is good and acceptable and perfect.
(Romans 12.1–3)

That is what following Jesus entails; and the renewal of the mind
comes close to the heart of the matter.

In this short passage there are all the elements that the newly
healed Naaman needs, whether in the ninth century BC or the
twentieth century AD.

This is how Naaman's two basic moves look today. First, present
yourself, your whole self (that's what Paul means by 'body',
actually), as a living sacrifice to God. Naaman carried home Jewish
soil so he could sacrifice to the true God on it. We are called to carry
Jesus with us wherever we go, so that at every moment of our lives
we may be offering ourselves to him as a living sacrifice. That is
what worship means. It must have focal points, corporate acts of worship, not least the Eucharist. But to stop there is to leave the glass
half full. You may need to start there, but don't stop there. Why not
fill up the glass, fill it to overflowing, with the glad worship of the
true God which consists in a whole life lived as an act of gratitude, of
glad self-sacrifice? That's the first thing: worship, worship that can be
flat on its face in adoration and up on its feet following Jesus
wherever he goes.

The second thing is to think straight about ourselves. 'Don't be
conformed to this world' – to the Rimmons, the false gods, the gods
that we worship by default, simply by being a member of a largely
pagan society. Rather, 'be transformed by the renewing of your
minds'. Naaman's thinking was turned inside out when God healed
him in the river Jordan. Our thinking is to be turned inside out when
we realize that the true God raised Jesus from the dead and thereby
announced to the whole world that he is the life-giving God, the God
of generous love, the God who takes the metaphorical leprosy of the
world and deals with it. Let the true God renew your mind as you
worship and follow his risen Son.

One of the signs that we are starting to think straight is that we
recognize, to our chagrin, that we are involved in all sorts of compromises and paradoxes. Some people think when they become
Christians that they are now perfect; that it's possible to live a pure
spiritual life, uncomplicated by the old realities. But that's not straight
thinking: it's just a new version of crooked thinking. Rather, when

someone comes to embrace the love of God in Jesus, or rather to be embraced by that love, they must begin to see that they are regularly and habitually bowing down in the house of Rimmon at several points in their everyday life. Anyone reading this book is most likely involved in some way in the economic and social life of the modern Western world, which, like every other human society without exception, is guilty of all sorts of injustice, and which dehumanizes some members of society in order to inflate the egos of others. This, though regrettable, is not controversial. What are we to do about it?

I suggest that as a first move we should do what Naaman did, and work forwards from there. It's no good trying to pretend we aren't compromised; we are. Nor is it any good imagining that we can cut the knot of those compromises all at once. We have to think straight about what we're doing, and own up to the compromises which at the moment we can't seem to avoid. When I bow myself down in the house of Rimmon; when I buy from a firm that may be paying its directors too much and its junior employees too little; when I use a bus that is polluting the atmosphere; when I find the pagan pressures too great and simply give in here and there; then, as Naaman said in the memorable phrase from the Authorized (King James) Version, 'the Lord pardon thy servant in this matter'.

The good news is that he does. Did Elisha say to Naaman: 'You're a half-hearted compromiser, you want your bread buttered on both sides at once, you're talking out of both corners of your mouth'? No. He said, 'Go in peace.' That is the word of God to those who are starting to bring their thinking about God and the world into the straight line that flows from the revelation of the saving love of God in Christ. It is the word of God to those who are starting to follow Jesus, and want to do so more and more. It is the word of God to those whose glass is half full.

That is why we say, as part of the regular Lord's Prayer, 'Forgive us our trespasses, as we forgive those who trespass against us.' If Jesus had expected us never to compromise again, he wouldn't have put that clause into the prayer. The key thing is, to recognize again and again that we need to pray it, and to pray it from the heart – and to go on working out how to eliminate those compromises bit by bit from our lives. Think again of Eliot's Magi: 'no longer at ease in the old dispensation'. Our minds are to be renewed; we can't be content with the old patterns any more. We may still have to live with the old world, but woe betide us if we are at ease in it, because it is still fatally possible that the glass might be half empty instead of half full.

The story of Naaman, which is actually a classic little comedy, gives birth at once to a very different story, which is its tragic mirror-image. We look, more briefly, at our second muddled man.

Here is Elisha's servant Gehazi. He has accompanied Elisha here and there, has watched as he did remarkable things, has stood by as Elisha called on the life-giving God of Israel and was wonderfully answered. If Gehazi was around today you wouldn't find him with the obvious pagans. He would be helping out in church. He would be sitting on committees doing good works.

But what has happened to his thinking? Has his closeness to the man who was close to the true God made him think straight? Alas, no. He thinks crookedly about Naaman: 'My master has let him off too lightly,' he thinks, in letting him go without paying. He sees Naaman as an enemy to be squeezed for what he's worth, not a child of God coming to be healed. This leads to a direct lie: he runs after Naaman and tells him a cock-and-bull story about two young men who need clothes and money. His lie forces him into deceit; he turns the messengers back in case Elisha sees them, and hides the money (and it was a lot of money) and clothes in the house. And the whole thing comes together in the big lie (5.25), which again comes out superbly in the old Authorized (King James) Version: 'And Elisha said unto him, whence comest thou, Gehazi? And he said, Thy servant went no whither.' Who, me? I'm clean.

No, Gehazi: you are compromised. And your compromise is not like Naaman's. Your glass is half empty, not half full. You have seen the living God at work, and you are deliberately choosing paganism, the worship of Mammon. You have seen the healing God at work, and you are deliberately choosing the way of sickness and death. You have seen the generous, loving God at work, and you have chosen the way of selfish greed. The punishment of Gehazi, in which Naaman's leprosy is transferred to him, is simply the ratification of the choice Gehazi has already made. He chose to think crookedly; and his twisted thinking about God and the world ended up distorting and destroying his whole life.

The story of Gehazi makes it quite clear that the story of Naaman does not mean that God doesn't care about compromise. Naaman says, what about me still going to the house of Rimmon? Elisha recognizes that he is moving gladly towards the light, and says, 'Go in peace.' His thinking has taken a large step towards being straightened out. Gehazi says, what about a bit of Mammon on the side? Elisha recognizes that he is moving eagerly towards the darkness, and exposes that darkness for what it is. His thinking is twisting itself into little knots. The true God is not himself threatened by the pagan gods; but those who claim to be God's people may still be so threatened. Those who want to follow Jesus must prepare to be tested.

I would like to think that there might be a few Naamans reading this book. If you're in doubt as to where you fit in the picture – whether your glass is half full or half empty – ask yourself this question. As you contemplate the resurrection of Jesus, what is your basic reaction? Christ is risen – so what? The sign of a Gehazi, with his glass half empty, is, first, boredom; then the question 'do I really have to take this thing that seriously?'; and then outright rebellion, answering 'no' to the question. The sign of a Naaman, of a glass half full, of a step towards the light, is the sense that in the resurrection the true God has revealed himself to be your God, and has called you to worship him, to straighten out your thinking with him at the centre, and to follow this Jesus along the way. You may have a long way to go. You will have to live for a while 'no longer at ease'. The change in your life may not be as dramatic as Naaman's. But if that's where you start you can take Elisha's words to Naaman as God's words to you: 'Go in peace.' And in that peace, with your mind renewed by the risen Jesus, start to think straight as you follow him.

CHAPTER NINE

Temptation

Whatever you do, don't even think about chocolate.

So: what are you thinking about? The subtle and sophisticated readers are thinking: I can see where this is going. The somewhat less subtle are thinking: obviously this is going to be a typical preacher's harangue. The less subtle still are, quite simply, thinking about chocolate.

So you see it's quite hopeless. Whatever I say is clearly going to be counter-productive. Telling someone not to yield to a particular temptation merely puts the idea of it into their minds, to be handled and fondled with interest and perhaps delight. This is so always and at all times. In the academic world, one is trained to see the other point of view, to take the opposite line and see where it goes. A distinguished academic once remarked gloomily to me that the best way to win an argument in his Governing Body was to argue on the opposite side, thus provoking one's colleagues to interested disagreement and luring them into the trap of supporting the position you really wanted them to take all along.

That's why, in dealing with the topic of temptation – which, as we saw in the previous chapter, is a vital one as we consider how following Jesus works out in practice – I don't simply want to say things which run along the surface, and which well-taught Christians have heard many times before. It is fairly obvious (for instance) that the story of Jesus' temptations in the wilderness (Matthew 4.1–11) has him dealing with the flesh, the world and the devil. One could explore that happily for a while. It is, likewise, pretty well standard fare to point out that Jesus succeeded where Adam and Eve failed. It's quite well known that he also succeeded where Israel in the wilderness failed, and indeed that Matthew intends us to focus on that in particular, since Jesus, like Israel, goes out into the desert after coming through the water, and since he uses as his principal weapons against the enemy texts taken from Deuteronomy, which is all about that highly ambiguous chapter in Israel's history. Lots of sermon potential there.

Or, taking a different tack, we could quite easily analyse Genesis 3 to see what went wrong, how the initial temptation succeeded. The serpent questioned God's command; Eve started to think things out for herself instead of trusting and obeying; once she got into an argument she was always going to lose. Likewise, we could quite easily analyse Matthew 4 and see what went right. Jesus stuck with Scripture and insisted on living it out, even when all his senses, and a good deal of wisdom and common sense too, would have gone along with the voice that pressed in on him, closer than breath itself. The preacher then has a fairly obvious time of it. Copy Jesus; don't copy Eve, still less silly old Adam who didn't even put up a fight but ate (knowingly, it seems) what Eve put in front of him.

And I suspect you would feel sad at a sermon like that. Most of my readers have been there, done that, and don't feel satisfied with it. Good advice might conceivably help, but it hasn't helped all that much in the past. Christians seem to me to divide into two groups these days: the first lot don't think that sin matters very much anyway, and the second know perfectly well that it does, but still can't kick the habit. So perhaps we need to look a little deeper, and set the question of temptation into its proper theological context.

One of the hardest things to get hold of in the Bible is the place of Satan. We think of this creature, if at all, as the arch-opponent. But it then comes as something of a shock, in the book of Job for instance, to discover that he's one of God's *servants*. Then, just as we're trying to get our minds round what that might mean, we discover that he's a *rebellious* servant. Curiouser and curiouser. We would like things to be simpler than that, wouldn't we? We'd like to live, ideally, in a world without evil; but, since that doesn't seem to be the case, we'd settle for a world where everything was clear cut. One of the reasons for the abiding popularity of watching sport is that we know from the start who's who. We emerge from the murky world where we live most of the time into the artificially bright light of a straightforward dualism. We support this lot; that lot are the enemy. If our lads are the underdogs, so much the better; we get a nice buzz of moral superiority, and it's all the nicer if we win against the odds. That's what we want life to be like. We watch sport because it allows us the luxury of a clear-cut dualism in a world where, for the most part, things aren't that easy. One of the disappointments of growing older, in fact, is the realization that nothing is as straightforward as it once seemed. Take politics, for example; or even church politics; though there are many who urge us to view both as if they were, preferring the quick certainties of youth to the humility of age. Fundamentalism, to that extent, is the attempt to do with religion what many do with sex, using it as a way of recapturing lost youth.

The trouble with most views of temptation is that we are always hoping that Christianity will be more like sport and less like real life. Preachers, in fact, often follow St Paul and appeal to an innate sporting instinct: there's a race to be run – and you want to win, don't you? That's fine when you're young and strong and there's an apparent chance that you *might* win. But what about when you're middle-aged and overweight and the very idea of running for anything except the odd bus fills you with a deep foreboding? You'll be happy to settle for second place, or even for thirty-second. And there are many Christians (including some who are still quite young in human terms) who are in exactly that position today. It all sounded so bright and cheerful and hopeful when we were in Sunday school; but the clear morning sky has clouded over now, and the choice seems to be between pretending it's still all clear and bright and shining, on the one hand, and settling in for a long grey afternoon, on the other. A choice, in other words, between an artificial, enforced, continuing childhood, and a gloomily realistic adulthood. Peter Pan on the one hand; Eeyore on the other.

And the reason I can't simply say the standard things about temptation is because I suspect that you'll read it in Peter Pan mode, and react to it in Eeyore mode. You will hear me saying that everything is clear cut: there's a straight choice between good and evil, and you've got to put on the spiritual armour and fight the good fight of faith. And you will go away thinking, 'That's all very well for him; my life is more complicated than that.'

So how do we break out of this cycle? How can we arrive at an analysis of temptation which gets closer to reality, and gives us a sight of what genuine, realistic victory might look like and feel like? How can we, in short, get to grips with the things that prevent us from following Jesus as, in our heart of hearts, we want to? There are three points which, I think, go to the heart of it.

First, temptation always takes as its starting-point something which is in itself good. The dualistic division of the world into good things and bad things simply won't do. There is such a thing as a distinction between good and evil, but we can never get at it by expressing it in terms of different parts of the created world. Chocolate is the creation of the good and loving God, just as much as bread. Sex, despite what you'd think to hear some people talk, was God's wonderful idea all along. Alcohol is such a great thing that Jesus once went to a wedding and made lots more of it. The human emotions, especially those of falling in love, are so wonderfully important that an entire book of the Bible is devoted to exploring and celebrating them. It would be bizarre if following the Jesus who made more wine for a wedding meant automatically renouncing alcohol and sex.

Is that dangerous talk? Only for a dualist, who wants everything black and white. A serious Christian will realize that sin comes not in the thing itself, but in its wrong use; not in a part of God's good creation, but in the attempt to use that good creation as though it were our toy, or our trash. When faced with temptation, Christians are often tempted, at a level far deeper than the surface temptation, to hate some part of God's good world; to hate, even, some part of their own bodies, or some part of their own psyche. We are tempted to regard the world, and even to regard ourselves, like a football match; we're on the side of some parts of ourselves, playing against other parts of ourselves. And the worst of playing that game is that you're bound to lose, and deep down you know it. But in fact (as we saw in the chapter on Colossians) it's not like that. Temptation always starts from something which is part of God's good creation.

What then, second, about the 'flesh', and all that biblical stuff about the flesh being at war with the Spirit? That's all true, too; but 'flesh' in that context doesn't mean this physical material we're made of. It's often been pointed out that most of the 'works of the flesh' listed by St Paul could perfectly well be practised by a disembodied spirit – anger, jealousy, malice, and so forth, and especially pride, spiritual pride. What 'flesh' means here is not physicality, but a human being in rebellion against God. That's the key. The temptation which feels as though it's appealing to the 'real you', to your deepest instincts and longings, is in fact starting from something which is good, and suggesting that you elevate that out of its proper and God-given context into a different setting where it will give you a thrill, rather than the God-designed satisfaction; a shot in the arm, rather than sustenance for the long journey. What feels like a part of the real you is in fact the habit that we get into of rebellion, of using our God-given world, our God-given personalities, and our God-given bodies, as if they were simply ours to use and abuse as we like, to give an artificial boost to our flagging self-esteem.

The answer to temptation, thirdly, cannot be to say that the thing offered is bad in itself. If you go by that route, there are only two destinations. The first destination, for those who seem to be succeeding, is a spiritual pride accompanied by a continuing spiritual immaturity. You will have achieved the goal of living as though parts of you, as though parts of the world, didn't exist; that may give you quite a buzz of satisfaction, but it gives God no pleasure at all, seeing that you're denying the first article of the creed, his good and wise creation of all that is. The second destination, for those who try but fail, is paranoia, self-hatred, a sense that one must be the worst creature that ever existed, the feeling that everybody else is all right and only I am a mess. Pride and fear are the ugly sisters waiting to greet us down those roads.

No; the answer to temptation is to find out, perhaps painfully and over a long period, what it is about you that is at the moment out of shape, distorted, in pain. Then one may begin to find out, again often painfully, how it is that God longs to help you to get what is distorted back into focus; to get what is crooked back into shape; to get what is bruised and hurt back into health. That will take time; it will certainly take prayer; there is good reason to think it may also take fasting. There is excellent precedent for saying that you will need help. Wise spiritual and practical guidance is part of your birthright as a member of the body of Christ. To try to follow Jesus and battle with temptation, without realizing that this is really what it's all about, is like trying to play football when your feet are tied together with a chain. To grapple with temptation knowing that its roots run deep into the person that you presently are is to engage with it realistically. Someone who starts there will never make the mistake, made classically by strict Christians from a variety of backgrounds, of confusing necessary self-*denial* with paranoid self-*hatred*. Nor will they be likely to make the mistake made by those on the rebound from this first one, to give up self-denial because one has learned to give up self-hatred. A good deal of would-be rewritings of the Christian moral code occur along exactly that line.

In the mean time, while you're working on the long-term project, what about the temptation which will creep up on you before you're even started? The first thing to do is to thank God for making you human; for giving you life and all that it means; for giving you responsibility to think and choose. The second is to pray for grace to use that responsibility wisely. The third is to recognize that every moment, every second of your life, is a moment when the gracious God longs to give you the good gift of his presence and his love, and has some specific response from you which he longs to evoke, which will enrich and enhance your humanness in the way that rebellion never can. If you don't follow Jesus in this precise moment, you are going to miss out. Often the sharpest temptation comes at the critical moment, when God is waiting to bring you round a corner to some unexpected blessing or gift. In the light of all this, and in the power of the Spirit, make your choice, and act on it gladly, giving thanks to God.

And if you fail, God's love does not. That love can be grieved; that love can never go away. It is that love, ultimately, that is our chief weapon against temptation. To know that I am loved, loved deeply, through and through, gives me the security to reject the ways of pride and fear; to reject the false alternatives of Peter Pan and Eeyore; to choose the way of self-denial which is also the way of self-affirmation, and to reject the way of self-hatred which leads not to holiness but to despair. To know this love, and to act out of answering love, is one of the central features of following Jesus. And, as we choose, we will find, like Jesus in the wilderness, that, to our surprise, angels may come and minister to us.

CHAPTER TEN

Hell

There was once a woman who was a brilliant musician. When she died, she gave her two most prized possessions to her two grandchildren. To the first, she gave her violin; to the second, her piano. The first, who had been learning the violin for some years, gradually transferred from her own instrument to the old, much-loved one. Eventually, she could play it just like her grandmother had done. The second, who likewise had had piano lessons for some while, went on playing his own piano. He put the splendid old piano in the best room in the house, where it looked fine, but gradually went out of tune. Nobody noticed when woodworm set in, until it was too late, and it was chopped up for firewood.

If you have ears, then hear.

Following Jesus is not merely a nice religious option for those who care to try it for size. As the previous chapter made clear, it may demand tough choices. We prefer, naturally, to talk about the pleasant side of Christianity. But the whole Christian tradition is clear that among the reasons for following Jesus there is the question of the alternative to be considered. If we don't follow Jesus, as persons and as communities, what results can we expect?

Ultimately, it only makes Christian sense to talk about comfort if it also makes Christian sense to talk about discomfort. Otherwise we water down the Christian message into bland and benign platitudes, cutting off the heights as well as the depths in a way that carries no resonances in the rich literature of Judaism or Christianity, but smacks rather of the cool and complacent world of the eighteenth-century Enlightenment, to which (alas) we still find ourselves in bondage. How can we, like the children of Israel, break out of this intellectual slavery, and grasp the full message again? How can we in particular, today, grasp the significance of what the Church has said down the years about the awful possibility of final loss, of human beings failing to reach the goal for which they were made?

There are three initial points to be made as we circle round this tricky topic and try to get to grips with it.

First, it must be said as clearly as possible that as soon as we find ourselves wanting to believe in hell we find ourselves in great danger. The desire to see others punished – including the desire to do the punishing ourselves – has no place in a Christian scheme of things. There is, of course, a right and proper desire for justice, for the victory of right over might; the desire to punish, however, must be sharply distinguished from this. And justice, when it comes in this world, may well involve some sort of retributive action against the perpetrators of injustice. But punishment for its own sake, as it were, is something else. Philosophers and psychologists, as well as theologians, have debated the nature of punishment for years without getting very far, but one thing seems to me clear: that if I find myself *wanting* to see someone else in torment, I am plucking from the tree a fruit which is sweet for a moment but bitter for an hour, and which will poison me unless I repent. All too often such desire stems from jealousy rather than justice, from fear rather than fairness, from repressed guilt rather than a longing for the kingdom of God.

Second, most of the passages in the New Testament which have been thought by the Church to refer to people going into eternal punishment after they die don't in fact refer to any such thing. The great majority of them have to do with the way God acts *within* the world and history. Most of them look back to language and ideas in the Old Testament, which work in quite a different way from that which is normally imagined. Let me give you an example. When Jesus speaks, in Mark 13, of the sun and the moon being darkened, and the stars not giving their light, we imagine today that he's talking about the end of the whole space-time universe, resulting in a cosmic judgement. But the language is taken from Isaiah 13, which is not about the collapse of the universe, but is rather a prediction of the cataclysmic fall of Babylon, the great city that has been persecuting the people of God. Jesus' re-use of this language is true to the genre. It refers, not to the collapse of the universe, but to the fall of Jerusalem. As a historian, I can say categorically that Jesus' language about the awful punishment in store for those who rejected his message must be read as predictions of the awful future that awaited the

nation of Israel if she rejected the way of peace which he was propos-
ing. When he spoke about 'Gehenna' he was talking about the
Jerusalem rubbish-dump – a great, foul, smouldering heap. His warning was that those who persisted in going the way of nationalist rebellion rather than the way of peace would turn Jerusalem into a huge
and foul extension of its own rubbish-dump. The warning came true.

So from these two points – the danger of our wanting to send
people to hell, and the fact that most of the New Testament warnings
aren't about that anyway – we may already deduce that there is some
serious rethinking to be done, for which of course we don't have
space within the confines of a single chapter in a book which is really
about something else. My third point is a preliminary one about that
rethinking, that reconstruction.

When the Bible speaks of human beings and how they order or dis-
order their lives, the assumption is that we are all made in the image
of God. This gift, however, is not a right, an automatic possession; it
is the gift of God himself. It is like a wonderful instrument
bequeathed to us by a loving parent or grandparent. And the way to
keep the wonderful instrument in tune is to play it – to play it for all
it's worth; to practise reflecting the image of God, which you do
through worship, and love and service to one another, rejoicing with
the joyful and weeping with the mourners. You do it, in other words,
by following Jesus.

But if we worship other gods – and the other gods are very powerful and active in our world right now – then all we can expect is for
the image to atrophy. The instrument will go out of tune. We won't
notice that woodworm has set in until it's too late. That's what Jesus
was saying to the Jews of his day. Get the instrument back in tune
now, or not at all. Horrific judgement – this-worldly judgement, the
devastation of cities and the tearing apart of nations – will follow the
decision to go on worshipping other gods. For us, the warning should
be equally clear. We, after all, live in a world where devastated cities
and large-scale human tragedies are reported every day in the news-
papers, and nobody seems able to do anything about it. There is such
a thing as forgetting what it really means to be genuinely human. It is
dangerously possible to start reflecting gods other than the true God
in whose image we were made. But the other gods are not life-giving.
To worship them, and to reflect their image, is to court death: the
eventual utter destruction of all that it means to be truly human. If we
doubt it, we need only watch the news.

There, then, are my three initial points. First, beware the desire to punish. Second, read the New Testament warnings as what they are, not as what they aren't. Third, recognize that it is possible to worship gods other than the true one, and so to cease being truly human. As we move on from there, we must look at two levels of human life, the personal and the social.

First, the personal. I think we are becoming more aware in our own generation of just what a delicate and sensitive instrument a human being really is. We go out of tune very easily. We need handling with care. But we are pretty hopeless, much of the time, at doing this. We need to learn to respect the image of God in ourselves and in one another. If we don't, as all around us we see people not doing, then we daily and hourly become less than truly human. The instrument needs regular tuning and playing if it is to stay as it should. Without that, there is nothing in the Bible or in Christian tradition to deny the possibility that individual humans can progressively choose to be less and less genuinely human, until they eventually cease to be human at all. But how are we best to think about this?

In the last century there was an acrimonious debate between those who insisted that we must believe in the eternal punishment of the damned and those who insisted on what is called 'conditional immortality', that is, the granting of immortality only to those who are saved, and (as the other side of the same coin) the annihilation of those who are not saved, so that they pass not only beyond the reach of hope but also beyond that of pity. The latter proposal was an attempt to do justice to the insight, which grew up quite suddenly in the nineteenth century, that no Christian can feel anything other than genuine pity for a lost human being who is conscious of being lost; and that *a fortiori* God must feel a similar pity. But if a creature has simply ceased to bear God's image at all, has ceased to be human at all, then pity becomes inappropriate. Sorrow at a loss, yes; but not pity.

My way of addressing this question is different. It seems to me – and I should stress that this is a personal opinion advanced tentatively – that if it is possible, as I've suggested, for human beings to choose to live more and more out of tune with the divine intention, to reflect the image of God less and less, there is nothing to stop them finally ceasing to bear that image, and so to be, as it were, beings who were once human but are not now. Those who persistently refuse to follow

Jesus, the true Image of God, will by their own choice become less and less like him, that is, less and less truly human. We sometimes say, even of living people, that they have become inhuman, or that they have turned into monsters. Drugs can do that to people; so can drink. So can jealousy. So can unemployment. So can homelessness, or lovelessness. I don't believe, myself, that any living human being ever quite loses the divine image. But that some seem to work towards it as though (so to speak) hell-bent on it seems to me beyond a shadow of doubt.

I see nothing in the New Testament to make me reject the possibility that some, perhaps many, of God's human creatures do choose, and will choose, to dehumanize themselves completely. Nor do I see anything to make me suppose that God, who gave his human creatures the risky gift of freedom and choice, will not honour that choice, albeit through the deep sorrow and sense of loss that any God we can truly imagine must carry at his heart, a sorrow lived out fully on Calvary. This, I think, is the way in which something like the traditional doctrine of hell can be restated in the present day.

This sombre thought is not, however, where I believe we should place the greatest emphasis if we are to do justice to the New Testament. If there is a proper, though difficult, biblical doctrine of hell in terms of final individual human destiny, there is an equally proper and yet more necessary biblical doctrine of hell in terms of human social and corporate life on this earth. And, indeed, if we were to concentrate on the former – the question of personal destiny – we might easily slip into the dangerous position of ignoring the latter. Those who talk all the time about eternal destiny can easily be lulled into using such talk as an excuse for forgetting the first major climax of the Lord's Prayer: 'Your kingdom come . . . on earth as it is in heaven' (Matthew 6.10). And if we forget that, we have ceased to be followers of Jesus. As Christians, we look for the marriage of heaven and earth, not their separation; and in that light we must look with Christian realism at the possibility of a different, and disastrous, marriage, which has become all too real a possibility in our own day: a marriage of hell and earth. That is what Jesus warned about in his own day. We can do no less in our own.

What does this disastrous marriage look like, and how does it come about? Its early stage – the diabolical courtship stage, if you like – occurs when a society quietly begins to sit loose to the true worship of the true God and begins to worship other gods. We passed that point in Britain some time ago. Its developing mode is seen quite clearly when some parts of society put their own interests ahead of the needs of other members of the same society. That's where we are at the moment: we have reduced the rate of inflation at the cost of inflating the rate of dehumanization in our society. For every point inflation has gone down, unemployment and homelessness have gone up in their thousands. Dividends earned by the rich are paid for, often fairly directly, by Third World countries who are struggling simply to pay off interest, not even yet capital, on the huge debts they have incurred through no fault (very often) of their own. We spend billions on smart missiles, and in the same breath we shut hospitals. These are the signs of a courtship between earth and hell that is already well advanced. The engagement stage, at which point firm commitments are made and it becomes hard to break off, is when vested interests, confronted by the dehumanizing results of their own policies, declare brassily that that's just too bad. Jesus warned his hearers that they should be ready to read the signs of the times. What would he say to our times today? What should his followers have to say?

If the diabolical marriage is to be called off – and if it isn't, then we really are in for hell on earth – it is time, now, to call a spade a spade, to name idolatry for what it is, and to set about opposing it with all the tools at our disposal. If Jesus opposed it, those who follow him can do no less. And if we are to do this it cannot simply be by making denunciations. We must offer, as well as a sharply-aimed critique, a true word of comfort. The Advent message, read each year from Isaiah 40, speaks the word which we need both to hear and to speak:

> Comfort, O comfort my people,
>   says your God.
> Speak tenderly to Jerusalem,
>   and cry to her
> that she has served her term,
>   that her penalty is paid,
> that she has received from the Lord's hand
>   double for all her sins. (Isaiah 40.1–2)

To a generation in exile, the prophet brought God's word of comfort. Our own generation is in an exile so deep that it often can't even see how bad its own condition is. But the message still rings true. Comfort, O comfort my people, your God keeps on saying – keeps on saying it, over the babble of the bureaucrats and the Eurocrats, over the shrill exchanges of the money-makers, over the slamming of doors behind those thrown out on the street, over the sad footsteps of those walking away from a lost job. Comfort, O comfort my people: our God does not intend that his children should live for ever in exile, he does not wish that we should make for ourselves a hell on earth. He is the God who brings in the kingdom of gentleness and justice, feeding his flock like a shepherd and carrying the lambs in his bosom. He is the one whose word is spoken, as a voice crying in the wilderness, warning us to get ready a pathway for our God. As John the Baptist warned, the axe is laid to the roots of the tree, and if it's already worm-eaten it will fall all the quicker. Let us take heed, and celebrate with fear and delight the coming of the one who will judge all things. Let us, in following Jesus, be prepared to announce as he did the message of comfort and discomfort, of welcome and warning. And let us, in our own day, so turn from our sins, individual and corporate, so worship the one in whose image we are made, and so follow the Image himself, that we as individuals and as a society may live out the prayer we pray, the prayer for hell to be vanquished, and for heaven and earth to become one.

CHAPTER ELEVEN

Heaven and Power

Where has heaven gone to? A few years ago John Lennon, in a famous song, invited us to imagine it didn't exist. It was a seductive invitation, not least to a generation tired of heavy-handed certainties and ripe for a counter-culture. Like a lot of English people, Lennon's idea of the meaning of 'heaven' seems to have been that which you'd get if you followed the line taken by a lot of hymns which are sung at Ascensiontide:

> Lord, though parted from our sight
> Far above the starry height,
> Grant our hearts may thither rise,
> Seeking thee above the skies.

This is following Jesus with a difference. Sophisticated Christians will quickly say that all that sort of language is simply metaphorical. It doesn't mean that Jesus has literally gone to some place in the solar system millions of miles away. But an awful lot of people on the edge of the Church, and outside looking in, still imagine that Christians are committed to believing something like that, and they of course find it incredible.

Worse: they find it oppressive. This idea of 'heaven' has been used to back up exploitation on the one hand and dry-as-dust moralism on the other: because this strange distant place exists, and because you might want to go there yourself some day, you'd better behave nicely here – which often means, you'd better sit down, shut up and don't be a nuisance. Lennon was reacting against a notion of heaven and hell that he saw as a myth designed to keep middle-class morality comfortably in power, and people like himself uncomfortably on the edge, powerless, impotent and angry. So he said, in effect: heaven is for the birds – let's get on with living here and now.

The protest may have been justified, but it was in reality an exercise in missing the point. The two major themes of Ascensiontide, the season where these problems seem to emerge most obviously, are precisely heaven and power; and the claim is that the ascension of Jesus radically challenges all normal human notions of both those things. Our society is still as muddled about them as it was when Lennon sang his song. We need, as Paul says in Ephesians, to have fresh wisdom and insight in knowing things as they truly are, so that we can grasp the true nature of the Christian hope and inheritance, and the genuine Christian concept of power, which challenges all other human ideas of power. In addition, having looked in the last chapter at the way in which failure to follow Jesus leads to hell, both here and hereafter, it is no bad thing to balance this with a serious look at the meaning of heaven itself. If that's where he's gone, his followers had better get their minds round it.

'Heaven' is, in fact, one of the most misused religious words around today, with the possible exception of the word 'God' itself. The biblical notion of heaven is not of a place far away 'way beyond the blue'. Nor is it simply, as some have said in reaction to that older notion, a state of mind or heart which some people can attain here and now. Heaven is God's space, which intersects with our space but transcends it. It is, if you like, a further dimension of our world, not a place far removed at one extreme of our world. It is all around us, glimpsed in a mystery in every Eucharist and every act of generous human love. We are reminded of it by the beauty of the created order, which in its very transience points beyond itself to the fuller beauty which is God's own beauty, and which he intends one day to bring to birth, as we say so frequently, 'on earth as it is in heaven'.

The Christian hope is not, then, despite popular impressions, that we will simply 'go to heaven when we die'. As far as it goes, that statement is all right; after death those who love God will be with him, will be in his dimension. But the final Christian hope is that the two dimensions, heaven and earth, at present separated by a veil of invisibility caused by human rebellion, will be united together, so that there will be new heavens and a new earth. Heaven isn't, therefore, an escapist dream, to be held out as a carrot to make people better behaved; just as God isn't an absentee landlord who looks down from a great height to see what his tenants are doing and to tell them they mustn't. Heaven is the extra dimension, the God-dimension, of all our present reality; and the God who lives there is present to us, present with us, sharing our joys and our sorrows, longing as we are longing for the day when his whole creation, heaven and earth together, will perfectly reflect his love, his wisdom, his justice, and his peace.

The ascension of Jesus, then, is his going, not way beyond the stars, but into this space, this dimension. Notice what this does to our notion of heaven. The Jesus who has gone there is the human Jesus. People sometimes talk as if Jesus started off just being divine, then stopped being divine and became human, then stopped being human and went back to being divine again. That is precisely what the ascension rules out. The Jesus who has gone, now, into God's dimension, until the time when the veil is lifted and God's multi-dimensional reality is brought together in all its glory, is the human Jesus. He bears human flesh, and the marks of the man-made nails and spear, to this day, as he lives within God's dimension, not far away but as near to us as breath itself.

This means, contrary to what some might suppose, that a doctrine of heaven focused on the ascension can never be used as a way of oppressing people, or of diminishing the value of their humanness. On the contrary; it affirms the true and lasting value of being human. The risen Jesus was more human, not less, than he was before: his risen humanness is the affirmation of his previous humanness, only now without the frailty and the dying which before then he shared with the rest of us. His resurrection is thus God's way of saying that there is such a thing as genuine humanness, that human life is not a Sartrean sick joke, promising everything and giving nothing.

But, if this is so, the ascension is the affirmation that God has taken that fully human, deeply and richly human being Jesus, and has embraced him to himself within his own dimension, his own space, making him indeed Lord of the world. God always intended that his human creatures should inherit the world, the created order, to rule over it with wisdom and gentleness, to bring it order and to enhance its beauty. In the ascended human Jesus that vision is in principle realized. There is always a risk that by talking of Jesus 'going to heaven' we allow a false picture of heaven to colour the image we now have of Jesus. What I am suggesting is that, instead, the true image of the human Jesus, the very Jesus we are called to follow, should subvert our false pictures of heaven, and should become the centre of the true picture instead.

If we can get that point straight, then our notions of power should find themselves radically altered in turn. So much of our contemporary life, as has of course been true in every human generation, is concerned with power. Who's in power, who's out of power, who has the power to do this or that; these are the questions that seem to matter. We jostle for power, we are angry with people who manipulate us because they have power and we don't. Money is important chiefly because having it gives you power. Even sex is valued, partly at least, because it seems to give you power over someone else. Nietzsche taught us not to trust what people say, because again and again they are trying to exert power over you. We have learned this lesson, and become a generation of cynics, seeing power-ploys behind every seemingly innocent action. And even cynicism itself can be seen as another attempt to wrest power from those who seem to have it. We live in an age that is dying for power, and that is in fact dying *of* power. Marriages become power-games, and both partners end up losing, to say nothing of the children. Nations grasp their freedom, and at once, as we have seen, fragment into power-hungry factions. The much-vaunted modern Western economic system puts a heavy gloss on what's going on, but underneath it's not far from the scramble for power described in Golding's *Lord of the Flies*. What should the follower of Jesus do in a world like this?

Over against the love of power, the ascension of Jesus sets the power of love. The great court-scene which comprises Daniel chapter 7 (on which, see chapter 3 above) is all about power. In Daniel's vision, the last great monster who has come up from the sea stands up in the courtroom and speaks out great arrogant words, great boasts about its power. Like all human empires before and since, the monster, which represents the height of human wickedness, babbles on about all the things it can do. Like all human empires, the supreme thing it can do is to kill.

But God, presiding over the courtroom scene, silences the monster's arrogance. Instead, he exalts to his own right hand one like a son of man, a human figure, and gives dominion, authority and kingly power to him. But this is not the same sort of power as that which the monster had exercised. The Church is often tempted to think it can simply beat the powers of the world at their own game, by using the cross as a symbol of earthly victory. Followers of Jesus sometimes imagine that the victory of their cause is all that matters, whatever means they use to that end. But that is a travesty of the whole meaning of the ascension, and of the cross and resurrection which give to the ascension its depth and resonance. God's exaltation of Jesus vindicates not only him and his cause, but his *way*; and that way is the way by which his followers too must walk.

The original writer of Daniel, and those who studied the book at the time of Jesus, interpreted the 'son of man' figure to refer to the faithful few who suffered for God's sake at the hand of the tyrants, and who would be vindicated at the last. Jesus drew this image on to himself, and went to his death believing that thereby the power of the monsters would be broken, the weight of human arrogance would have done its worst, and that then the creator God, the God of love and new life, would vindicate him and so begin the process of establishing his own kingdom, in which power has been stood on its head. The chief thing that the monsters can do, then and now, is to kill. Jesus believed in a God who could, and would, raise the dead.

The power of God, says St Paul in 1 Corinthians 1, is therefore revealed in human weakness, supremely in the weakness of Jesus. At the heart of the Christian gospel stands the ridiculous paradox that true power is found in the apparent failure, and the shameful death, of a young Jew at the hands of a ruthless empire. Why? Because there are more dimensions to reality than just the ones we see and know in our own space and time. Heaven, God's space, is the present but unseen reality. And, in that all-important dimension, the crucifixion was not a defeat but a victory; in the death of Jesus, as we saw in chapter 2, the powers of evil were themselves being judged, were being put to shame, were being decisively rebuked for their arrogance. Instead, the generous self-giving love of Jesus, giving himself for the sins of the world, has been vindicated and exalted as the supreme principle of the universe. More: Jesus himself, no abstract principle, but a human person, is now exalted as the still loving, still giving, still generous Lord, to whom one day every knee shall bow, and whom we are today summoned to follow.

A nice dream? No; more than that. A good idea now disproved by the continuance of human wickedness? No; that's not the point. The twist at the end of the story comes when St Paul writes (Ephesians 1.20–3) that the power which raised the crucified Jesus from the dead, and which exalted him in triumph in God's own space, ruling over every other authority and every human power – this same power is what God now wants to exercise through his people. The victory of Jesus over the evil in the world is not simply a *fait accompli* which could be disproved by the continuance of evil to this day. It is a victory *waiting to be implemented through his followers*.

A moment's thought will show that it could not be otherwise. Precisely because God's power is not manipulative, does not crush or squash human beings, but rather ennobles and fulfils them, God now longs that we, his children, should take our own part in implementing his victory, the victory of the power of love over the love of power, throughout his creation. Those who commit themselves to following the ascended Lord Jesus are thereby signing on for this task.

The areas in which we are called to do this are as many as the areas of human concern. We must work and pray that the power of love, the wise and gentle and healing rule of genuine humanness, will be exercised over the created order. The alternatives are not attractive: the arrogant grasping love of power, on the one hand, and on the other the ugly pantheism which wants to worship the earth itself instead of its creator. It's not too demanding, however, to speak of large issues like these. It's every bit as important that we learn the power of love in our own relationships, forswearing all manipulation and domination, and giving ourselves away to others in risky but generous love.

The great empires of the world, as Napoleon said in a moment of candour, depend on force. They have come and gone; and the ones that now exist will follow in their turn. They make fear and death their weapons, and they themselves die when the fear they have generated turns into violent rebellion. Jesus, at his ascension, was given by the creator God an empire built on love. As we ourselves open our lives to the warmth of that love, we begin to lose our fear; and as we begin to lose our fear, we begin to become people through whom the power of that love can flow out into the world around that so badly needs it. That is an essential part of what it means to follow Jesus. And as the power of that love replaces the love of power, so in a measure, anticipating the last great day, God's kingdom comes, and God's will is done, on earth as it is in heaven. We will not see the work accomplished in all its fullness until the last day. But we will, in following Jesus, be both implementing his work and hastening that day.

CHAPTER TWELVE

New Life – New World

So what happens to people after they die? Where do followers of Jesus end up, so to speak? One passage from an early Jewish writing which has been very popular and influential through Christian history is found in the Wisdom of Solomon, which speaks of the souls of the righteous being in God's hand: *Iustorum animae in manu Dei sunt*. It's a well-known passage, often set to music:

> The souls of the righteous are in the hand of God,
> and no torment will ever touch them.
> In the eyes of the foolish they seemed to have died . . .
> but they are at peace. (Wisdom 3.1–3)

This passage is often taken as evidence that the writer didn't have any idea of a future resurrection; all he was interested in was the immortality of the soul. Many Christians, if pushed, would probably agree. But can you really be a serious follower of Jesus on that basis?

There has, of course, been a great debate about resurrection and immortality. People have often tried to water down the Christian hope into a vaguer, less specific, certainly less embodied, doctrine of mere immortality, 'survival'. Orthodox mainstream Christianity has always responded that what we believe in is more than mere immortality. Even though it's difficult for us to get our minds round it, there will be a new sort of physicality, a new embodiedness, for which the only appropriate language is that of resurrection, the raising of bodies to new life.

Why do we believe that? And what does it matter what the Wisdom of Solomon says, when it's not even in the official canon of the Old Testament? Well, the Wisdom of Solomon was a very influential book around the time of Jesus. Reading it helps us to see what some people at the time were thinking.

Actually, however, the passage in Wisdom has been woefully misunderstood. If you read only the first two or three verses, the famous and often-quoted bits, you get the distinct impression that it's just talking about immortality: righteous souls being at peace in a disembodied existence, with God somehow looking after them there. But in fact that's only part of the story. The righteous have died, and the wicked think that's the end. No, says the writer, God has them safe, at peace; but then, as he goes on from verse 7, 'in the time of their visitation they will shine forth, and run like sparks through the stubble; they will govern nations and rule over peoples, and the Lord will reign over them for ever'. Now that's not just immortality: that's resurrection. It's a renewed world with renewed people in it.

What the writer is saying is that the righteous dead are, *for the moment*, safe in the keeping of God, at peace, out of sight. But that's not the end of their story. A temporary rest, followed by a new life in the kingdom of God. And the kingdom, or kingship, of God is not, at this period, just an airy-fairy idea. It speaks of a this-worldly restoration in which justice and peace will be established for ever. The righteous rest in peace, in order to rise in glory. This, I suggest, is what is promised for the true followers of Jesus.

Now the purpose of all this, apart from helping us to understand a much-quoted and much-misunderstood passage, is to lead directly in to the first main thing I want to say in this chapter, which is this: that *the word 'resurrection' means what it says*. The first followers of Jesus used it most emphatically to describe something that had happened to Jesus, which had had the effect of making them his followers in a quite new way. Hitherto, they had followed him in the hope of national renewal, of the fulfilment of Israel's great hopes. Now they followed the one whom they believed to be the risen Lord of all, of the whole world. Without the resurrection, we can't understand the very reason why anyone would have continued to follow Jesus after his death.

Within first-century Judaism, the great majority of Jews kept a firm grip on their hope for national restoration. God would visit his people, and would restore their fortunes, not by taking them off into a world of disembodied bliss, but in a thoroughly this-worldly way. Therefore, as they realized, the righteous men and women of old, long since dead, would have to rise again to share in this glorious new reality. It wasn't a matter of those currently alive going off to join those who were now in a disembodied heaven; rather, those who had died long ago would return to join those who were still alive when the great day dawned. If what you hope for is the *renewal* of this world, rather than the *abandonment* of this world, then resurrection follows naturally.

What such Jews thought would happen, in a nutshell, was that their God, the creator, would perform a great triple act of renewal: renewal for the nation, for the world, and also for the righteous dead. 'Resurrection' was part of a package deal, a great total renewal. It *could only mean* that people who had been emphatically dead became emphatically alive again.

And the question of Easter – the question which is I think simply dodged by those who declare that we can't believe in the physical resurrection of Jesus now that we have modern science and the electric light – is therefore this: what sort of event must have taken place to cause a bunch of first-century Jews to start talking excitedly about 'resurrection', and claiming that it had actually happened? What sort of event must have taken place to cause those early disciples to declare that the great renewal, the great reversal, had begun to take place; that God's kingdom was now in principle established; that God was pouring out his Spirit on all flesh, renewing his whole creation? What must have happened to make them talk like that?

My argument is that something must have happened which *forced* those disciples, despite their hopes having been dashed when Jesus was crucified, to declare that Israel's hope, resurrection, had already happened, because it had happened to him. Most of what they had hoped for quite obviously hadn't happened at all. Israel had not been liberated; the Romans, in the person of Pontius Pilate, were still ruling Judea; injustice and oppression were still on the loose. How could they possibly say that the great new day had dawned? Something must have happened. And it must have been something to do with Jesus being alive again, in a sense close enough to the ordinary sense for them to be shocked into making this quite stupendous claim.

Historically, we are in the following position. Imagine standing by a river. A road runs up to one bank of the river, and stops at the water's edge. As we look across the river, we see that there's another road starting on the opposite bank. Then we see a car, which we saw on this bank half an hour ago, now parked on the other side. There is no bridge in sight. The sensible hypothesis is that there is some sort of ferry which took the car from one side to the other.

In the case of Easter, the expectation of first-century Jews is like the road on this side of the river; the existence of the early Church is like the road on the other side. First-century Jews talked about resurrection: the early Church claimed that it had happened. Why? The only solution which will really fit the evidence we have is that what they said was true. Jesus was indeed raised bodily from the dead on Easter morning.

Other solutions have of course been tried. They had a sudden strong feeling that God loved them even after they'd run away and abandoned Jesus. They thought that Jesus' mission and work should continue even though he was dead and gone. Jesus had taught them about a supernatural, non-physical kingdom of God, and after his death they concluded that he had gone on ahead into that other realm. They were ignorant first-century peasants and didn't know the laws of nature that say dead men don't rise. And so on.

Frankly, none of these will get the car over the river. The word resurrection, and all the other concepts that cluster around it, simply doesn't mean any of those things. It has to do with the blunt belief that someone who was physically dead is now physically alive. The Jews had language for forgiveness, for great experiences of knowing the love and forgiveness of God, for continuing the work of a great prophet, and even for believing in a supernatural world after death. Jesus' followers didn't use that language. They talked about resurrection. They knew as well as we do that dead people don't get up again. It blew them away as much as it does us.

Resurrection, then, means what it says: not survival, not the immortality of the soul, not eternal disembodied bliss, but bodily resurrection. Jesus seems – and the New Testament writers are as aware as we are that they are at the edges of language at this point – Jesus seems to have gone *through* death and out the other side. His new life was not less than physical; but it seems to have had a new dimension to it as well, a kind of transphysicality, humanity with more dimensions added.

That is the first and most important thing I want to say. Resurrection means what it says, and we are right to affirm, in the plain sense of the words, that God raised Jesus from the dead. Had he not done so, nobody would have followed Jesus from that day onwards. A crucified Messiah, as we saw earlier on, is a failed Messiah. Why would anyone want to follow him at all?

The second and third things to be said follow from this, much more briefly.

To begin with, *we must build the resurrection into our thinking about what will happen to all of us*. Far too often today Christians slide back into thinking of the immortality of the soul, of mere survival in some shadowy existence, or of a disembodied heaven, as the ultimate destination of God's people. It's a measure of just how seriously the bodily resurrection has been taken within the tradition that Christians have asked the impossible question: do those who die go into a different time-sequence, so that they go straight to the ultimate destination at once? Or do they rest, and as it were 'sleep', while waiting, so that we all arrive at the end together?

Talking of 'going to heaven when you die', or of being 'in paradise', is in fact one way of answering that question: we go to rest and wait. 'The souls of the righteous are in God's hand, at peace.' But we wait for something more: for the new world, the marriage of heaven and earth and the renewal of both. Whatever you decide about the chronology of life after death, 'heaven' by itself is not the ultimate destination of the Christian. Heaven, or as some Jews called it, 'paradise', is a *temporary* resting-place, in between bodily death and bodily resurrection.

People who ask, 'What will heaven be like?' show, therefore, that they've missed the point. The ultimate destination of Jesus' followers is the renewed earth, which will be joined together with the renewed heaven, to make a world with extra dimensions – just as Jesus' new body seems to have had extra dimensions. When we speak of life after death, therefore, as of course we must both in comfort and in hope, let us school ourselves to speak of it Christianly, and not slide back into the half-light of mere 'immortality'. This is my second point: God's future for his people is a newly embodied life on a renewed earth, married to a renewed heaven. This is the hope that followers of Jesus must keep before their eyes.

But, finally, *the resurrection gives a vision not only of a new life, but of a new world*. Paul, in 2 Corinthians 5.17, spoke of it this way: 'if anyone is in Christ – new creation! The old things went away: look, they became new.' As the Archbishop of Canterbury has emphasized in recent statements, the resurrection is not an appendage, a doctrine you can stick on to a Christianity that exists independently of it. The resurrection of Jesus *is* Christianity. And this means that it becomes the starting-point for all Christian thinking and living, challenging all other possible starting-points. This is where Jesus' followers must orient themselves clearly if they are to follow him truly.

We have, first, a new reason to build for the kingdom. We can't build the kingdom by our own efforts; it will take another mighty act of our God to bring it in at the last. But we can build *for* the kingdom. Every act of justice, every word of truth, every creation of genuine beauty, every act of self-sacrificial love, will be reaffirmed on the last day, in the new world. The poem that glimpses truth in a new way; the mug of tea given with gentleness to the down-and-out at the drop-in centre; the setting aside of my own longings in order to support and cherish someone who depends on me; the piece of work done honestly and thoroughly; the prayer that comes from heart and mind together; all of these and many more are building-blocks for the kingdom. We may not yet see how they will fit into God's eventual structure; but the fact of the resurrection, of God's glad reaffirmation of true humanness, assures us that they will. In the sight of the foolish such actions seem to die, to be lost without trace; far better to live for oneself, to look after number one. But we can be at peace, and wait for the kingdom into which our present little efforts to build will one day be incorporated. That is what following Jesus is all about.

Second, followers of Jesus have a powerful reason to choose holiness. I hear a good deal of talk these days about 'wholeness' and personal fulfilment. Many Christians speak of this as though it were completely self-justifying; as though self-fulfilment is *the* thing above all that matters. Of course God desires to reaffirm all that is truly human within us, including our bodies, our relationships, our work, our creativity. But the message we hear in Jesus is that this reaffirmation of humanness follows crucifixion; that wholeness is found down the road of holiness. 'Take up your cross,' Jesus said; he invites us to a great act of faith and trust, to look with a clear eye at the moral choices we face and to be prepared to say 'no', even if it really hurts, when faced with subtle and powerful temptations. In the sight of the foolish, such behaviour seems to be death; but we will be at peace. We are to live in the present as resurrection people: 'if you have been raised with Christ,' says Paul, 'seek the things that are above . . . [and] put to death . . . whatever in you is earthly' (Colossians 3.1–5).

That's never easy. In fact, it's always exceedingly painful. But the resurrection gives the followers of Jesus a powerful reason to go that route: because the resurrection promises that our bodily humanity is to be renewed and restored. Our bodies are not just toys that we will throw away at death, and which we can therefore do what we like with now. Nor are they miserable rags, worthless and hence morally insignificant. Our emotions, and those of others, are not just chance flickerings of an electric current that will one day burn itself out and prove irrelevant. Our humanness is precious; God takes it so seriously that he has promised to bring it out, as it were, in a new edition. Despite what some may say, the real incentive towards genuine holiness, towards taking up our cross and following Jesus, comes not from fear of punishment but from a clear understanding of what it means to be human. And we only get that clear understanding when we grasp the truth of the resurrection.

Finally, the resurrection gives us a powerful reason to worship, and so to follow, the risen Jesus. If it is true that Jesus has been raised from the dead, he is not just a private cult-figure, not just someone that Christians happen to know in some private way. He is the Lord of the world. Paul got into hot water in Thessalonica for declaring that there was 'another king named Jesus' (Acts 17.7). In the world of his day, language like that was treason. It meant that Jesus called into question the absolute power claimed by Caesar, the absolute no-questions loyalty that Caesar demanded. That was what the kingdom of God meant; that was what following Jesus involved. In our world, we would have to diversify the claim: there is another Prime Minister; there is another Vice-Chancellor; another Lord Mayor. More: there is another starting-point for thinking and living, which neither the market economy, nor Freudian psychology, nor international power politics, nor anything else in our present hierarchy of ideologies, can touch. And we have the privilege of worshipping and following this Jesus, this King. The resurrection opens up before those who would follow Jesus a new life, a new world. And that new life and world, though they will be fulfilled in the life yet to come, begin here and now.